TELEPEN

D1426073

EUGENE

By the same author:

Plays Volume 1
(The Lesson, The Chairs, The Bald Prima Donna, Jacques)

Plays Volume 2
(Amédeé, The New Tenant, Victims of Duty)

Plays Volume 3
(The Killer, Improvisation, Maid to Marry)

Plays Volume 4
(Rhinoceros, The Leader, The Future Is In Eggs)

Plays Volume 5
(Exit The King, The Motor Show, Foursome)

Plays Volume 6
(A Stroll In The Air, Frenzy For Two)

Plays Volume 7
(Hunger And Thirst, The Picture, Anger, Salutations)

The Bald Prima Donna (Typographic Edition)

Past Present: Present Past
(Thoughts and Memories of Eugene Ionesco)

PLAYS
VOLUME VIII

EUGENE IONESCO

HERE COMES A CHOPPER

THE OVERSIGHT

THE FOOT OF THE WALL

Translated from the French by
Donald Watson

CALDER AND BOYARS

LONDON

First published in France
by Editions Gallimard Paris

ⓒ Editions Gallimard Paris

These translations first published in Great Britain 1971
by Calder & Boyars Ltd
18 Brewer Street London W1R 4AS

ⓒ Calder & Boyars 1971

ISBN 0 7145 0760 1 Cloth Edition
ISBN 0 7145 0761 X Paper Edition

Printed by photo-lithography
and made in Great Britain at
The Pitman Press, Bath.

CONTENTS

HERE COMES A CHOPPER   7

THE OVERSIGHT   101

THE FOOT OF THE WALL   115

HERE COMES A CHOPPER

HERE COMES A CHOPPER was first performed as JEUX
DE MASSACRE at Le Théâtre Montparnasse, Paris, on
September 11th, 1970, with the following cast:

HOUSEWIVES - Lucie Arnold, Mäia Simon, Michele Loubet,
Liliane Rovère, Claude Génia, Paulette Frantz, Josine
Comellas, Zouk: MEN IN THE STREET - André Thorent,
Philippe Mercier, Alain Janey, Dominique Bernard, Raymond
Jourdan, François Viaur, André Julien, Gilles Guillot:
DIGNITARY- Raymond Jourdan: MASTER OF THE HOUSE -
Andre Thorent: SERVANTS - Dominique Bernard, Alain
Janey, Paulette Frantz, Michele Loubet: KATIA - Lucie
Arnold: ALEXANDER - Francois Viaur: JACQUES - Alain
Janey: EMILE - André Thorent: PIERRE - Andre Julien:
THE NURSE - Liliane Rovère: THE DOCTOR - Philippe
Mercier: 1ST CITIZEN - Raymond Jourdan: 2ND CITIZEN -
Dominique Bernard: NURSE - Josine Comellas:
PRISONERS - Gilles Guillot, François Viaur: JAILER -
Alain Janey: PASSER-BY - Zouk: COMPANION - Liliane
Rovere: JEANNE - Liliane Rovère: JEAN - Philippe Mercier:
LUCIENNE - Mäia Simon: MOTHER - Josine Comellas:
SERVANTS - Michele Loubet, Claude Génia: TRAVELLER -
André Thorent: DAUGHTER - Mäia Simon: WOMEN - Zouk,
Paulette Frantz, Liliane Rovère, Lucie Arnold: YOUNG
MAN - Gilles Guillot: ELDERLY PEOPLE - Alain Janey,
André Julien: NURSES - Claude Génia, Michele Loubet:
MAN - Dominique Bernard: POLICEMEN- François Viaur,
Philippe Mercier, Raymond Jourdan: 1ST ORATOR - Alain
Janey: 2ND ORATOR - André Thorent: CHARACTERS - The
rest of the company: POLICEMEN - Philippe Mercier,
Raymond Jourdan: OLD MAN - André Julien: OLD WOMAN -
Claude Génia: PUBLIC OFFICIAL - Raymond Jourdan:
WOMEN - Paulette Frantz, Liliane Rovère, Mäia Simon,
Michele Loubet, Lucie Arnold: MUTES - Dominique Bernard,
Alain Janey, Gilles Guillot: BLACK MONK - André Cazalas

The play was directed by Jorge Lavelli

SCENE ONE

(The scene is the town square. Neither a modern nor an
ancient town. This town should have no particular character.
The most suitable period would be between 1880 and 1920.
Market day. Plenty of people about, if the theatre is a
large one. Not nearly so many, if the theatre is a small
one. A few can be made to appear many, if the cast
available is carefully disposed or if the same characters
appear and reappear in different hats, with or without
umbrellas, sometimes wearing and sometimes removing
their beards. These people walk about in silence for quite
a long time. They look neither gay nor sad, they have
either been or are just going shopping.

Before the entrance of any of the characters who seem to
be coming from the market, we will have seen this at the
back, with people buying and selling. The hum of
conversation and bustling, busy sounds.

It is very colourful. Bells.

If there are not enough actors, it would be just as good, or
even better, to have puppets or large dummies instead.
These figures can be made to move or not, according to
whether they are real puppets or just painted figures.

At the end of this first scene, if they are real puppets they
can turn and face the public, motionless, with a look of
anguish, or perhaps be staring at that part of the stage
where the action is taking place. If they are fixed dummies
or painted figures, they can just fade into the greyness
(which will also happen anyway with real puppets, for the

stage will be cloaked in semi-darkness at the end of the
scene and you will only see their silhouettes moving through
the mist.

Before the appearance of the 1ST and 2ND HOUSEWIVES,
also entering from the right a few paces ahead of them, a
character they do not notice will simply cross the stage:
a very tall, black-robed and hooded MONK.

The 1ST and 2ND HOUSEWIVES come on from the right)

1ST HOUSEWIFE. This disease is only caught by monkeys.

 (Exit the MONK)

2ND HOUSEWIFE. I'm glad to say we keep dogs.

1ST HOUSEWIFE. And cats.

2ND HOUSEWIFE. But the virus is carried by people, who
 pass it on.

1ST HOUSEWIFE. Deliver it by hand? They can't do that on
 purpose!

 (They go out)

3RD HOUSEWIFE. My husband told me most of these people
 have no particular morals. That's why they die. They
 live incoherent lives.

4TH HOUSEWIFE. Needs must when the devil drives!

 (They go out. The 5TH and 6TH HOUSEWIVES could be
 the 1ST and 2ND with some change of clothing: a
 different shopping basket, with or without an umbrella,
 carrying a different coloured basket, etc... All this of
 course depends on the number of people and props
 available in the theatre and on what can be provided for
 the production: just another reminder that a crowd can
 be created with 50 people or 11)

1ST or 5TH HOUSEWIFE. (entering from the Left, with
 one other) In the old days you really had to scrub the
 carrots. If you didn't they'd give you leprosy.

10

6TH or 2ND HOUSEWIFE. Nowadays potatoes give you
   diabetes or make you too fat. Spinach is bad, creates too
   much blood. Lentils give you colic. And if you cook
   them, no more vitamins, no more enzymes, and that
   kills you. Alcohol's bad for you, makes you alcoholic.
   Water's no better, even in gum boots. You get frogs in
   your tummy, and gurgle and croak.

5TH HOUSEWIFE. Meat's bad for you. Uric acid. And fish
   makes you hopping mad.

6TH HOUSEWIFE. Fish makes you hopping mad?

5TH HOUSEWIFE. Because of the phosphorus. Makes them
   jump like crackers.

6TH HOUSEWIFE. What, crackers in the head?

5TH HOUSEWIFE. And mussels can cause the plague! And
   oysters and shellfish.

6TH HOUSEWIFE. My husband won't touch asparagus, bad
   for the kidneys. He knows. He's a doctor. He's got
   patients with asparagitis.

5TH or 1ST HOUSEWIFE. But aubergines only give you
   colds.

6TH or 2ND HOUSEWIFE. The plague's more fun than that.

   (They go out. Enter the 3RD and 4TH HOUSEWIVES)

5TH HOUSEWIFE. Oh yes! Aubergines are cancerobscene.

   (The 3RD and 4TH or 7TH and 8TH HOUSEWIVES
   enter)

7TH HOUSEWIFE. My husband told me one day there'll
   be people who go way up to the moon. And higher than
   that.

8TH HOUSEWIFE. They'd need a ladder that's far, far
   bigger than a fireman's. And upside down, because the
   moon it seems downside up. As from every side it's

round, it must be round the other side.

7TH HOUSEWIFE. That's the point. Since it's seen from the earth on every side, why can't it be on our side?

8TH HOUSEWIFE. That's the risk. How many days would they need the ladder?

7TH HOUSEWIFE. They'd never make it. They'd run out of breath.

8TH HOUSEWIFE. They could do it in relays, with platforms on the ladders.

7TH HOUSEWIFE. Think how giddy they'd get! Heads or tails, up or down, you get giddy all the same.

8TH HOUSEWIFE. They could go up by cannonball. They'd shoot up on horseback astride a cannonball.

7TH HOUSEWIFE. That would be fatal. There'd be too much air. They'd be too scared. They'd die.

(They go out. TECHNICAL NOTE: Instead of going off the HOUSEWIVES could walk round the stage)

*   *   *   *   *   *   *

(The dialogue that now starts is intended to alternate with the series of entrances and exits that we've already had from the HOUSEWIVES.

TECHNICAL NOTE: The men should have the same number of speeches as the women; if the men have more speeches than the women, the women's speeches will have to be increased, or vice versa, up to the moment when they all meet together in fright and astonishment when the first disaster occurs: the death of a man, or a woman, of several men, or several women. It is possible that all the characters who are on the stage at the start of the play die at the end of this section, that is to say after only a few minutes. So that you probably see them lying all over the stage. Do not forget the silent arrival of the BLACK MONK.

The 1ST and 2ND MEN enter from the Left)

1ST MAN. (to the 2ND) We're all idiots, I'm afraid. And we're governed by imbeciles.

2ND MAN. We ought to find a cure for that, but the cure's not to be found.

1ST MAN. Never mind. I'll find it for you. I'll find it whenever you like.

2ND MAN. We'd be much obliged. Knowledge is power.

1ST MAN. Knowledge and power are the two great faculties of the spirit. Of the spirit of man.

(They go out. TECHNICAL NOTE: If the theatre can only provide 4 HOUSEWIVES to play 8 roles, there must be 4 MEN to play 8 male roles. If it is possible to have 8 HOUSEWIVES then there must be 8 MEN also.

Enter the 3RD and 4TH MEN from the Left)

3RD MAN. (pushing a pram) On Sundays it's my turn to push the baby's pram. I've got twins and my wife knits.

4TH MAN. (knitting) With me, it's the other way round.

(They go out. The 5TH and 6TH MEN come in)

5TH MAN. I tell you things weren't going well at all. It was like being in a thick fog. I felt quite lost. Agitated. A sort of impatience in the muscles and the nerves. In fact things were going very far from well. I couldn't sit or stand or lie down. I could't walk because it made me tired. And I couldn't stay where I was.

6TH MAN. Still, there was one solution. Not a very nice one. But the only one.

5TH MAN. What was that?

6TH MAN. Hang yourself. You should have got yourself hanged.

5TH MAN. Dangerous.

6TH MAN. But worth the risk... It was far worse for me: depression. The whole world had become a distant planet, impenetrable, made of steel, remote. Something completely strange and hostile. No communication. Cut off. It was I who was shut up inside, yet I was the outsider.

5TH MAN. And where was the lid? Inside out or outside in?

6TH MAN. I couldn't lift it anyhow. It must have weighed tons. Tons and tons. Of lead. No, of steel as I said. After all you can melt lead!

5TH MAN. I've never been able to lift more than 60 kilos. And I prefer 60 kilos of straw to 60 kilos of lead. Straw's lighter, you know.

6TH MAN. Sometimes one wonders how one goes on living. Not always a bowl of cherries is it? As my friend Gaston says.

5TH MAN. Perhaps we'd be better off dead?

6TH MAN. Don't say that, it's bad luck.

(They go out on the Right. The 7TH and 8TH MEN enter)

7TH MAN. We're not the same race as those who race among the planets.

8TH MAN. We're the race that's racing to destruction.

7TH MAN. They're only highly skilled technicians. They'll go to the moon, they'll go to the stars. They'll go further than we shall. But they won't know more than we do. What sort of views will they have?

8TH MAN. More extensive than ours.

7TH MAN. Yes, but what will they know about the whole caboodle? They won't know a thing about the <u>whole</u> thing. And it's the whole thing that counts, the rest is nothing.

8TH MAN. That's true. Nothing counts for much. (A short pause) Still, I prefer top floors. The tenants on the top floors have a higher, wider view than tenants down below.

7TH MAN. Not always.

8TH MAN. How's that?

7TH MAN. If the building's on a hillside and the tenants on the top floors have their windows or their dormers or their spy-hole facing toward the hill, then even the topmost floors would seem like cellars and it's the others get the panorama. So the lower tenants get the higher view.

(They go out. Enter the 1ST and 2ND WOMEN)

1ST WOMAN. My brother-in-law is researching on unconditioned reflexes. That's harder than when they're conditioned.

2ND WOMAN. One can only do what one's asked. But <u>what</u> they ask!

(They go out. Enter the 5TH and 6TH MEN)

5TH MAN. I can feel joy rising within me. It seems like joy already. Trying to climb from my feet to my heart. But I'm afraid it won't get past the ants in my pants.

6TH MAN. I'm not asking for pleasure in life, old man. I'll settle for a state of neutrality. Just quietly sit and watch the show. No suffering for me.

(The 5TH and the 6TH MEN go out. Enter the 3RD and 4TH WOMEN and the 3RD and 4TH MEN. The MEN on the Left, the WOMEN on the Right, as always. The 3RD

15

and the 4TH MEN still have their knitting and their
pram. But now it is the MAN who had the knitting who
has the pram and vice versa)

3RD MAN. (to the 4TH) There is no future.

3RD WOMAN. (to the 4TH) Nothing to predict. Yet
prevention is better than cure.

4TH WOMAN. (to the 3RD) To be forewarned is to be
forearmed.

4TH MAN. (to the 3RD) But you can't foresee the unfore-
seen.

3RD WOMAN. (to the 4TH) You can't cure the unpreventable.

3RD MAN. (to the 4TH) Even when it's predictable.

4TH WOMAN. (to the 3RD) The incurable can't be cured.

4TH MAN. (to the 3RD) And the predictable can't be
prevented.

3RD WOMAN. Curare's not curable. It's a poison. There's
no antidote to that.

(The other characters troop onto the stage, the WOMEN
from the Right, the MEN from the Left, and keep more
to the corners of the stage without speaking or
pretending to speak. They should seem fairly relaxed,
just looking without moving. The very tall hooded
BLACK MONK, on invisible stilts as previously, comes
in and stands at the Centre of the stage, quite quietly,
without anyone appearing to notice him)

4TH MAN. (pushing the pram with the babies into the
Centre of the front part of the stage, the MONK being
behind him; to the 3RD MAN) Those are the bells at
the end of Mass. Let's go and drink our absinthe before
my wife comes out.

3RD MAN. (to the 4TH) She's meant to be meeting my wife
in the cake shop.

4TH MAN. (to the 3RD) Put your knitting in the pram. The babies won't eat it. (To the 4TH WOMAN) As you're a good neighbour, Madam, will you keep a brief eye on the babies?

(The 4TH WOMAN approaches, followed by the 3RD WOMAN)

4TH WOMAN. (to the 4TH MAN) Good morning!

3RD WOMAN. I've never seen your twins before. Everyone says they're so pretty.

4TH MAN. Don't wake them up, whatever you do! Just while I have a drink with my pal.

3RD MAN. We're just off for a drink together.

(Before the MEN leave, the WOMEN start leaning over the babies)

4TH MAN. Shan't be long, ladies!

3RD MAN. And thanks. Don't forget my knitting's there too!

4TH WOMAN. (looking into the pram) I was told your babies were blonde. They don't look very fair-skinned to me.

4TH MAN. (who had started moving off towards the back of the stage with the 3RD MAN) There's none so fair! Or so pink!

3RD WOMAN. (looking into the pram) They've turned purple. Gone all black. They're asleep.

3RD MAN. Turned purple?

4TH MAN. My children all black?

3RD WOMAN. (touching them in the pram) It looks as if they're cold. Not enough warm clothes.

17

4TH WOMAN. When you touch them, they don't move.

3RD WOMAN. (looking into the pram) They're cold as ice. Oh, good heavens!

4TH MAN. What on earth are you talking about?

3RD WOMAN. But they're dead.

4TH WOMAN. They've been choked to death. Oh!

3RD MAN. What?

4TH MAN. They're glowing with health. (He looks into the pram and utters a cry) Dead!

3RD MAN. (looking into the pram and uttering a cry) Dead!

(While the 3RD and 4TH WOMEN draw back in confusion, crying out loud, and the other characters begin to stir in agitation, the 4TH MAN shouts)

4TH MAN. They've been smothered, strangled! My children have been murdered! Who did it?

(The other characters, wide-eyed with astonishment, slowly approach the group of 2 MEN and 2 WOMEN round the pram)

1ST WOMAN. Who could have done it?

4TH MAN. I know who it was. This morning I asked my mother-in-law to look after them. She always had a down on my kids. Because she hates me. Has done for a long time. She always has.

3RD WOMAN. He says it's their grandmother!

3RD MAN. That's no reason for killing children!

4TH WOMAN. And their mother doesn't even know what's happened!

18

5TH WOMAN. Oh, that son-in-law of mine! I could have wrung his neck. But not the children's. Besides, they've hardly got one yet! My daughter wouldn't let me. But I can understand, in a moment of anger.

6TH MAN. It's shameful!

7TH MAN. It's worse than shameful!

5TH MAN. They've always been a danger, old women! Killers and poisoners!

4TH MAN. (to the 2ND WOMAN) It's you, mother-in-law, you killed them.

2ND WOMAN. It wasn't me, I swear it.

4TH MAN. Murderess! (He rushes towards the 2ND WOMAN, who falls to the ground)

3RD MAN. (to the 4TH) Don't take on so!

8TH MAN. (to the 4TH) She's innocent.

1ST MAN. She's dead.

3RD WOMAN. (to the 4TH MAN) Assassin!

1ST MAN, 2ND MAN and 5TH WOMAN. (to the 4TH MAN, as they all make threateningly towards him) Assassin! Villain!

4TH MAN. She just...fell down. I never even touched her.

8TH MAN. (looking at the 2ND WOMAN) She's turned purple, gone all black!

6TH MAN. That woman was a guardian angel to me. You'll pay for this. (He rushes at the 4TH MAN, knife in hand)

3RD MAN. (to the 6TH, trying to hold him back) But he said he didn't do it. She just dropped down dead.

19

(The 6TH MAN is quite close to the 4TH MAN. The 4TH MAN falls to the ground)

4TH MAN. (as he falls) Aaaah! I'm dead! (He falls prostrate, his arms crossed over his chest)

3RD MAN. (to the 6TH) You killed my mate. Assassin! Swine!

6TH MAN. It wasn't me, I missed him. He just fell down. He slipped.

2ND MAN and 5TH WOMAN. (after inspecting the 4TH MAN on the ground) Look! He's gone all black! He's turned purple!

8TH WOMAN. It's more than I can stand. Police! (She puts her hand to her heart) Aaaah! My heart! (She falls dead)

8TH and 3RD MEN. (to the 6TH MAN) Swine! Assassin! (The 5TH MAN and 7TH WOMAN step between them)

5TH MAN. He didn't do it.

7TH WOMAN. He said he just dropped down dead!

(Meanwhile, the 1ST and 2ND MEN as well as the 1ST, 3RD, 4TH, 5TH and 6TH WOMEN have been inspecting the corpse of the 8TH WOMAN)

1ST MAN. She's not moving.

3RD WOMAN. We really ought to call a doctor.

6TH WOMAN. Or the fire brigade. I'll go for the fire brigade.

(She walks towards the rear of the stage and falls to the ground)

6TH MAN. It wasn't me. I didn't do it. I swear I didn't.

(Surrounded by the 3RD, 5TH and 8TH MEN, and the

7TH WOMAN, he collapses. When they surround the 6TH MAN, the characters must, of course, leave an opening towards the public so that the 6TH MAN can be seen to fall. After inspecting the 8TH WOMAN on the ground, the 1ST and 2ND MEN, with the 1ST, 3RD, 4TH and 5TH WOMEN raise their arms to the sky as they stand round the WOMAN)

1ST MAN. It's not her heart.

2ND MAN. Perhaps it's her heart.

1ST WOMAN. She looks a very funny colour!

7TH WOMAN. (looking at the 6TH MAN on the ground) He's dead.

3RD WOMAN. It's a punishment from Heaven!

5TH MAN. Perhaps he's only fainted?

(The first group of characters surrounding the 6TH MAN, that is the 3RD, 5TH and 8TH MEN and the 7TH WOMAN, as the second group of characters surrounding the 8TH WOMAN, now approach each other, exclaiming: 'I must say it's amazing! I should never have thought it! They make a pretty sight! And all because they were wicked! They are guilty! They are innocent!')

7TH MAN. (indicating the 6TH WOMAN, who lies dead) She just fell down! She was going for the fire brigade. (He rushes over to the 6TH WOMAN) We must pick her up!

7TH WOMAN. Surely she's not dead too?

1ST MAN. It's all over now. We won't all kick the bucket!

7TH WOMAN. (taking the hand of the 6TH WOMAN) She's quite still! Dead! (She falls dead over the WOMAN)

1ST WOMAN. We're not surprised any more!

8TH MAN. We've got the habit by now.

(He crumples up over the 6TH WOMAN and the 7TH MAN. The nine remaining characters start running in all directions over the stage, shouting and wringing their hands)

1ST WOMAN. Mercy!

1ST MAN. It's the scourge! The great scourge!

3RD WOMAN. Mercy!

2ND MAN. I've been a thief!

5TH WOMAN. Lord, have mercy!

3RD MAN. I've been a parricide!

5TH WOMAN. I've committed incest!

5TH MAN. (collapsing in the centre of the stage) Pity, mercy, pity, mercy!

7TH WOMAN. Forgive me!

1ST MAN. This is hell! (He collapses on the Right of the stage, downstage)

1ST WOMAN. I want to right the wrongs I've done. (She falls on the opposite side to the 1ST MAN)

3RD WOMAN. I'm not so wicked, really! (She collapses beside the 1ST MAN)

2ND MAN. Where are you, my darling, my little darling? (He falls down beside the 3RD WOMAN)

4TH WOMAN. My inside! How it burns! (She falls down beside the 2ND MAN)

3RD MAN. I'm in such pain all over. And the pain I've caused! Oh, children, my children! (He collapses next to the 4TH WOMAN)

5TH and 7TH WOMEN. (still running from one side of the stage to the other) I don't want to! The pain's too bad!

5TH WOMAN. Husband dear, your lunch! It's not ready yet!

(They both collapse in the two opposite corners of the stage)

SCENE TWO

(A DIGNITARY of the town addresses the public)

DIGNITARY. Fellow citizens and strangers. An unknown scourge has been spreading through the town for some time now. It is not war, there are no assassinations, and we were living quiet and normal lives, many of us were almost happy. Suddenly, with no apparent cause, with no previous sign of illness, people have started dying in their houses, in the churches, at street corners and in public places. They have started dying, can you imagine that? And what is worse, these are not isolated cases, one death here, another there. If need be, we should have to accept that. But the number of cases is constantly increasing. Death is advancing by geometrical progression. The doctors, the historians, the theologians and the sociologists tell us that the cause is a scourge that comes in cycles, rarely but in cycles, one that has not been known for several centuries, and then in a different part of the globe. This scourge travels round the world and attacks the happiest of countries or towns, yes, when they are at their zenith, at the very moment when it's thought that there is nothing left to fear. On the last two occasions this terrible phenomenon was reported in places far away from here, in Paris and another city of antiquity, Berlin. In Sicily too, it seems, but we no longer have enough documentary evidence to know precisely whether it was Sicily or Argentina. That our turn should have come is inconceivable when one thinks that Brest is closer to these lands. There are houses where whole families have been wiped out. Brothers and cousins have been struck down at the same time by the same scourge, the same anguish, followed by the same mortal agony. Even if they live in entirely different districts. For a time it was thought this phenomenon could be explained by the revival or resurgence of old ancestral feuds between families, or within the same family, such as no longer exist in our peaceful modern days. But people have died not only in the same house but in houses far removed from one another, strangers have been dying at the same time, people unknown to one another. So it might just as well have been a feud between strangers. The theory that these deaths were coincidental has been abandoned. There were too many coincidences. People are dying haphazardly. I have gathered you together for the last time in this public place to tell you what is happening to us, and what is happening to us is incomprehensible. We are being overwhelmed by a deathly visitation that has no known cause. It is my duty to inform you that not only neighbouring countries but the rest of our own towns have barred their gates to us. Soldiers surround the city. No-one may enter now and you can no longer leave. Only yesterday it was possible to go. From now on it is as if we were caught in a trap. Fellow citizens and strangers, do not try to take flight, you will not escape the bullets of the riflemen who cover all the entrances and exits. We have need of all our courage and all our force of resignation. I also need strong men to dig the graves. All wasteland and building sites must be expropriated, for our cemeteries are already over-crowded. I ask for volunteers to stand guard over houses that are contaminated, to prevent any person entering or leaving. We need sworn inspectors to investigate into houses touched by sickness in order to verify whether it is this mortal disease or not. I ask for women investigators to determine the cause of death, even to examine the living, take note of any rash, eruption or swelling they may find and denounce the culprits to the police, so that they may be confined. Any suspects who enter the house will be shut up with the others inside. Be on the watch for suspects. Denounce them. In the public interest. We ask for surgeons, transporters of the dead, and layers-out, everyone owes a service to his fellows. Everyone must be ready to observe or bury his neighbour. We know of no remedy for this scourge. We can try to contain it, and in this way we may, perhaps, some of us manage to survive.

But let no-one count upon it.

Meanwhile, no more beggars, no more vagabonds, no more banquets. Public entertainment is forbidden. Shops and restaurants will stay open as briefly as possible in order to reduce the risk of propagation. If in fact it spreads by propagation. For it is possible that this scourge descends on us from heaven, like invisible rain which can pass right through our roofs and walls.

As I told you, there will be no more public meetings. Groups of more than three people will be broken up. By the same token it is forbidden to loiter. The inhabitants will have to circulate in pairs so that each may keep watch on the other, and report to the layers-out if he is smitten.

Return to your homes and let each one stay in his own house. Let no-one go out, except for the barest necessities.

On every contaminated house will be painted a red cross one foot high, right in the middle of the main door, with this inscription: Lord have mercy upon us! (He goes out)

SCENE IN A HOUSE

(Decor: an empty room. A character with gloved hands comes in, carrying a round chair with armrests, while another SERVANT, also in gloves, arrives carrying a small dais. In the centre of the right-hand wall the chair is placed on the dais. To the rear a very large window extending from floor to ceiling, and giving onto the street.

At the Back, on the Left, an entrance door.

The TWO SERVANTS go out and return with atomisers.

A third character, a WOMAN, comes in also carrying an atomiser.

These characters spray the walls, the chair, and the platform.

From a door on the Right another character comes in, carrying 2 small chairs, which are placed one on each side of the right-hand door. This is also a WOMAN. She sprays the furniture, the floor, the walls and the ceiling. Through the window one can see what is happening on the street: a half-naked, ill-shaven MAN can be seen, running across as much of the stage as can be glimpsed through the window, and shouting: 'Have mercy on me!' He disappears.

Next come TWO MEN dressed in black, wearing masks to protect their nose and mouth against microbes and holding bludgeons in their gloved hands. They chase after the shouting MAN.

The 1ST PURSUER raises his bludgeon to finish off the MAN, who must have collapsed in the street.

A cry is heard.

The 2 characters, one of whom was carrying a bludgeon and the other a stretcher, are seen bearing the body laid out on the stretcher, shouting: the one, 'Pestilence', the other: 'Make way, make way'.

The MASTER OF THE HOUSE arrives. He is a dark man; rather tall and thin, wearing a dressing gown beneath which he has a dark suit. He has a kind of cap on his head and is wearing gloves like the others in the hope of warding off the scourge. He seems scared and every now and again takes from his pocket a small bottle that he uncorks, sniffs at, recorks and puts back in his pocket, before repeating the whole process.

Through the window you can see a WOMAN in rags running in the opposite direction from the MAN we saw just now: she will disappear shouting: 'Save my soul! I have killed my child'. She is followed by the same

PURSUERS, who will bring her back on a stretcher
shouting, the one: 'Pestilence', the other: 'Make way',
although there is no-one else to be seen in the street.
One can also see a MAN in policeman's uniform, who,
having consulted his list and checked the number of the
house, takes a piece of chalk from his pocket and draws
an enormous red cross on the door opposite.

Some MAN tries to open the door from the inside. The
POLICEMAN threatens him with his revolver and says:
'Forbidden to leave the house'. The door is closed again.

We shall see the MAN appearing at his window and see the
POLICEMAN strike him, so that he falls back inside his
house like a character from Punch and Judy.

All this latest business, from the time when the shouting
WOMAN appears, takes place after the first appearance
of the MASTER OF THE HOUSE on stage. These scenes
take place simultaneously, and others too perhaps, with
the scene inside the house.

The MASTER OF THE HOUSE watches his SERVANTS,
who are busy spraying in order to disinfect the place)

MASTER. Fumigate, purify, disinfect! We shall be safe
here. Who has the purifying perfumes?

1ST SERVANT. I do, sir.

MASTER. Who has the oil that prevents the scourge?

2ND SERVANT. I do, sir.

MASTER. Don't forget to smear one single joint. Hurry
up. Spraying is not enough. And the resin? And the
powders? (To one of the TWO WOMEN) Rub them in
everywhere. And the benjamin, the resin, the
insecticides, the sulphur?

1ST SERVANT. Here they are, here they are. We're rubbing
them in. (He rubs)

2ND SERVANT. Here's the sulphur, we're rubbing it in!

27

(He rubs)

MASTER. (to the 2ND SERVANT-GIRL) Bring me my
meal. Has the furniture been well polished and oiled?

1ST SERVANT. Yes, sir. With the product you recommended.

MASTER. (to the 2ND SERVANT-GIRL, who is going out)
Before you touch the dishes, put your white gloves on.
(To the 1ST SERVANT-GIRL) See that incense is
burnt. Near the door, by the window and in the corners.

(The SERVANT-GIRL obeys while the others go on
rubbing and disinfecting the floor, the walls etc. The
2ND SERVANT-GIRL brings in a tray with dishes for
the MASTER OF THE HOUSE, who goes to sit down in
the chair with armrests)

(Smelling the dishes as he settles himself) It still smells
of fish. It still smells of fruit. Have you added enough
prophylactic? You should have put more. We have to
take nourishment, but it's dangerous and we can't afford
to taste our food any more.

1ST SERVANT. If the weather wasn't so hot, the epidemic
wouldn't be so fierce.

2ND SERVANT. There's been all that hot rain too.

1ST SERVANT-GIRL. When we come to the snow and ice,
that'll soon drive it away.

2ND SERVANT-GIRL. They've stopped tolling the bells for
the dead, sir. There are too many of them. There
isn't the time.

1ST SERVANT. That's to reassure the population.

1ST SERVANT-GIRL. There are no bellringers left. Three
quarters of them have died of the disease.

MASTER. Why must you come so close? You'll stifle me.
It's more hygienic to keep your distance. Have you
sealed the doors? Have you sealed the windows?

28

(They move away from the MASTER OF THE HOUSE)

2ND SERVANT. You couldn't even slip a needle under the door!

MASTER. There shouldn't be room for a thread!

2ND SERVANT-GIRL. Everything's shut tight.

MASTER. We have wheat and rice, fish and smoked meat, we have dried fruits, we have nuts. And we are safe from the rats. (To the 1ST SERVANT) We'll have to inspect the roof. We can't have the wind lifting up a single tile. Needless to say, no-one's to come in or go out. We're safe here. Don't look through the window. A mere glimpse of the scourge may contaminate you. (He brings a morsel of food to his mouth) Have a good look, now. I can feel a slight draught. The wind carries the germs of the sickness. There may be no cracks now, but there might be. They could develop. The winds and the air press against the walls and the barriers, and try to penetrate. Be vigilant. Stop up all the holes with that wax. Always carry it with you. Go on, look round, inspect! Go on, go on!

(The 2 MALE SERVANTS and the 1ST SERVANT-GIRL hunt everywhere, stopping up the cracks or pretending to: there is great activity in the house. Only the 2ND SERVANT-GIRL stays near the MASTER OF THE HOUSE and serves his food.

Meanwhile, through the large window one can see a MAN in black carrying a black flag, who as he passes is followed by a cart bearing a coffin. A GUARD with his halberd walks behind the coffin. He is blowing on a trumpet and breaks off periodically to shout: 'Keep away'. According to the facilities available, the use of the cart is optional. If there is none, there will be 2 MEN in black carrying the coffin.

The MASTER OF THE HOUSE speaks while he eats, but he is eating with care, inspecting and sniffing each piece of food, so that there are some morsels he puts back in the plate without having touched them)

29

Stop up everything. Putrid air can come in through gaps that just appear. Atomise too. And don't be afraid to spray the food. Who cares if it has a nasty taste! You must go on spraying. For although the walls are thick, an evil wind can find its way in by magic. An evil spirit doesn't always acknowledge the presence of walls and barriers. He is invisible and matter does not exist for him.

1ST SERVANT. If you think about him, sir, he may get in through your thoughts.

MASTER. (shouting) Then think that he can't get in! Think that he can't! If the walls are hermetically sealed, the heart too must be staunch. The scourge will not enter this house, if you do not wish it. It will not touch you. But carry on with the fumigation. Go on checking for any gaps or cracks. See that none get bigger. That they're all stopped up again. There is no universe outside ourselves. We are impenetrable. That's what you must tell yourselves. Are we impenetrable? Answer!

1ST & 2ND SERVANTS. (still rubbing and fumigating) We are impenetrable.

MASTER. (to the 1ST SERVANT-GIRL) You must say it too!

1ST SERVANT-GIRL. I am impenetrable. The scourge cannot touch me.

MASTER. (to 2ND SERVANT-GIRL) And you?

2ND SERVANT-GIRL. The scourge cannot attack us.

THE FOUR SERVANTS. (together) The scourge cannot reach as far as us.

MASTER. I am impenetrable. I am untouchable.

(The MASTER OF THE HOUSE upsets the tray of food and falls flat on his face. The SERVANTS are terrified and rush towards him. The 1ST SERVANT-GIRL lifts up his hand and then lets it fall)

1ST SERVANT GIRL. The palms of his hands are turning
   black.

1ST SERVANT. (lifting his MASTER's head by the hair)
   His eyes are going red! His face is blue!

2ND SERVANT-GIRL. He's knocked everything over! He's
   broken the plates! And I haven't any more!

2ND SERVANT. (to the 1ST) These are the signs of the scourge.

1ST SERVANT-GIRL. These are the signs of the scourge.
   (Alarmed, all the SERVANTS abandon the body and rush
   to the door. They open it)

A POLICEMAN. (gun in hand) You cannot leave a house
   of sickness. If you try, I shall shoot.

(He takes aim at them and the SERVANTS fall back. The
door is shut noisily behind them from outside. They
rush to the window and try to break the glass. Another
POLICEMAN is there, armed. The SERVANTS recoil.
They are clearly frightened of one another. While the 4
SERVANTS, each in a different corner of the room, fall
on their knees, dark heavy shutters are placed against
the window from outside. Darkness invades the stage)

NEW SCENE

(ALEXANDER, JACQUES, EMILE, KATIA, THE
DOCTOR, THE NURSE. Decor: a bedroom in a clinic.
A window at the rear. The partition walls Right and Left
are glazed. Small door on the Right. On the Left,
ALEXANDER in his bed. 3 or 4 chairs. ALEXANDER is
about 60 years old, KATIA is a great deal younger. EMILE
and JACQUES are a little younger than ALEXANDER.
When the curtain rises ALEXANDER and KATIA are on
the stage with EMILE and JACQUES, who have just
arrived)

ALEXANDER. (to JACQUES and EMILE) Sit down. The
   chairs aren't very comfortable.

31

EMILE. (to ALEXANDER) It's nearly twenty years since I last saw you. And now you're ill.

ALEXANDER. But not dead yet.

EMILE. I know. You're working hard. Someone told me. You're writing an important new work.

JACQUES. I've read some extracts from it. It's excellent.

EMILE. What a ridiculous quarrel!

ALEXANDER. A misunderstanding.

EMILE. As you say, a misunderstanding. It has deprived me of your friendship for so long. But now I've found you again...

KATIA. He wasn't hard to find. You should have tried.

EMILE. (to KATIA) Why yes, of course. Alexander could have made a gesture towards me too.

KATIA. Against your will?

JACQUES. (trying to be conciliatory) He could, you know, Katia.

EMILE. (to KATIA) You're French, from Normandy. Why is your first name Russian?

ALEXANDER. Her first name is French, it's the diminutive form that's Russian. She christened herself with it. She was very fond of Chekhov.

EMILE. That's absurd. One can forgive almost anything, but one can't forgive anyone for having different ideas from oneself. A man who thinks differently is an enemy.

JACQUES. (to EMILE) That's because you have no vocation for friendship. Friendship is stronger than ideologies. You yourself have changed, you have adopted new ideas. Who does not change?

EMILE. For me, a friend is someone who thinks as I do. And to remain a friend, when I change my ideas, so must he. I'm half joking of course. But on the whole I mean it. (To ALEXANDER) I came to talk to you, to explain myself, to explain and understand a little, to discover the secret cause of our disagreement. Because since you changed your ideas you've changed them back again. For about ten years now you've had the same ideas as I have, but we still went on not seeing each other.

KATIA. (to EMILE) Don't tire yourself thinking too much. And what's more, don't tire him. The doctor doesn't want him to get tired. He was very doubtful, you know, whether to allow this visit.

ALEXANDER. Let's talk of something else. I'm glad to see you. Let's talk of nothing.

EMILE. There was one odd coincidence, though. We quarrelled the very day after I received that prize for literature.

KATIA. Alexander is above such things.

ALEXANDER. That's ridiculous!

EMILE. It's obvious. Alexander is not jealous. Perhaps he just disagreed ideologically with the members of the jury. Had it not been for that, they would surely have given him the prize. He deserved it more than I did. I mean, at the time, perhaps he thought I would give up the prize. That's what he'd have done himself.

KATIA. Definitely. He'd never have accepted it.

ALEXANDER. It's not unpleasant to spend a few months in a clinic. It's difficult at first. Then you get used to it. I live in an antiseptic world. The noise and fury of the world outside is toned down by the time it filters through to me. It's no longer frightening, or should I say so disturbing?

EMILE. Before we came in, we were sprayed with disinfectant.

33

JACQUES. Many people are dying at this time.

EMILE. More than usual. Lots of people die in the streets. They just collapse. The men tug off their ties, the women utter a cry, and then they die.

JACQUES. It's a fashion.

ALEXANDER. I know, I know what's happening.

JACQUES. (to ALEXANDER) Well, you're feeling better, aren't you? You're looking extremely well.

ALEXANDER. (to JACQUES) So are you. Although you're out in the streets all day, rushing round the town.

EMILE. (to KATIA) I wonder if you're not a little to blame that I stopped seeing Alexander. Remember? I had come round to your little flat for dinner, and afterwards, in conversation, suddenly... Why yes, I could see by your face you weren't pleased.

KATIA. I don't remember.

EMILE. Oh yes, you must.

JACQUES. (to EMILE) You must have got the wrong idea.

ALEXANDER. (to EMILE) You attached too much importance to it. One always attributes too much importance to things.

EMILE. Still, from that moment there was a distinct change in your attitude towards me.

JACQUES. (to EMILE) Don't tire him. You've said enough now, haven't you?

EMILE. If I'm tiring anyone, it seems to me it's Katia.

ALEXANDER. Since then we've done many things, but we were pressed for time. We had to move fast.

EMILE. Things had to be said when people were still

disposed to listen to us. Now they wouldn't listen. They have other preoccupations. All these deaths to start with.

ALEXANDER. (to EMILE) You're right. What we have to say has to be said straight away. That is how one finds a niche for oneself in the expression of opinion. We have only one word to say. It will get buried with millions of other words, but it will once have made itself heard. If one doesn't move fast, the word is no longer comprehensible, it loses significance, becomes out of date.

JACQUES. Every now and then works from the past are rediscovered and revived.

(The DOCTOR comes in, followed by the NURSE)

DOCTOR. (after approaching ALEXANDER with the NURSE at his side) Are you feeling better?

ALEXANDER. I still have this pain, but it's not so bad.

KATIA. (to ALEXANDER) You said you weren't suffering any more.

DOCTOR. (to the NURSE) Give him the injection.

(While the NURSE gives the injection, the DOCTOR turns to JACQUES and EMILE)

Stay seated. I have a lot of work at the moment. Today about a thousand people died in the streets of the same sickness.

JACQUES. One after the other?

DOCTOR. There are some who die one by one, others die in batches of ten or twelve. Science is helpless. We don't know what this strange epidemic is. There are no early symptoms. We can't treat anyone. And the autopsies reveal nothing.

NURSE. (to ALEXANDER) I didn't hurt you too much?

ALEXANDER. Now I feel much better. Better than I've

35

ever felt before.

KATIA. (to ALEXANDER) And you're usually such a martyr.

DOCTOR. Anyway, I must go back. I'm expecting another cartload to arrive. And the autopsies have to be done all the same.

NURSE. The number rises every day.

JACQUES. (to the DOCTOR) But you're still hoping for an explanation and a way to fight the disease?

DOCTOR. Is that what it really is?

ALEXANDER. Oh my friends! My friends!

KATIA. What's the matter?

EMILE. What did he say?

JACQUES. He said 'my friends'.

NURSE. (to the DOCTOR) Don't go. Look, his eyeballs.

ALEXANDER. My friends! (He has half risen in his bed. He falls back)

NURSE. He's fainted.

(The DOCTOR goes up to ALEXANDER)

DOCTOR. He's dead.

KATIA. Impossible. But he is. What am I going to do without him?

EMILE. And I never managed to talk to him. Too late!

JACQUES. His last words were: 'My friends!'

DOCTOR. (to KATIA) No, Madam, he didn't die of the illness he came here to be cured of. It wasn't the injection either.

EMILE. Why did he say: 'My friends'? What did he mean by
that? He sat up in bed, he wanted to tell us something
important.

DOCTOR. (to the NURSE) Close his eyes. Call the orderlies.
His body must go down to the morgue.

MEETING IN THE STREET

(1ST CITIZEN and 2ND CITIZEN. The two CITIZENS
come onto the stage at the same time, one from the Left,
the other from the Right)

1ST CITIZEN. Well, if it isn't you! Not dead yet?

2ND CITIZEN. I'm not a spook. It amazes me sometimes not
to be dead. But the fact is that I'm not. I exist, I still exist.

1ST CITIZEN. Still living in the 21st District? What brings
you here? We were informed your District was one of the
worst infected by the disease. Even worse than the 25th
District. Though less than the 27th. I thought I asked
for boundaries to be established, barriers to stop people
from the insalubrious areas coming in and trying to take
refuge in the less infected Districts. Especially mine.
The 1st. How were you able to slip through? I had this
regulation drawn up myself, approved by the majority
of the Town Council.

2ND CITIZEN. I'm not doing you any harm.

1ST CITIZEN. You are, you know, and I'm off straight
away to warn the mounted police.

2ND CITIZEN. I came into your District for the good of
the city. I've been appointed to see to provisions. Now
the sale of fresh fruit has been forbidden, I have to lay
in a supply of compote. Here's my pass and my mission
orders.

1ST CITIZEN. I shall inspect your permits...at a distance.
And your family?

37

2ND CITIZEN. Some are still alive, others are not.

1ST CITIZEN. How did a resident of the 21st District come to be entrusted with the provisioning of the city? Stand back. Speak to me at a distance of three yards, five yards even, so I'm out of range of your microbes.

2ND CITIZEN. And your family?

1ST CITIZEN. Nobody has been ill at home or died. No suspected case has been reported in any of the twelve houses in my street.

2ND CITIZEN. No-one can know what tomorrow may bring.

1ST CITIZEN. Nothing will happen to me. Or my family. No, no, don't come any nearer. You're from a very unhealthy place.

2ND CITIZEN. You seem very confident. Where does this assurance come from, this curious carefree air, just at a time when disaster is ravaging, decimating the town?

1ST CITIZEN. Nothing mysterious. The people who are ill, the dead and the dying were or have been careless. It's simply a question of not mingling with the crowd. Of not going near the sick. You simply have to do as I do, and keep away from all those who, like you, even if not ill, have been in contact with the sick. It's simply a matter of not mixing with the wrong people.

2ND CITIZEN. And if you were a doctor, a nurse or an undertaker's mute, what would you do?

1ST CITIZEN. I would resign. Besides, that's not the case. The only money I touch is from stocks and shares. I leave the risky jobs to other people. I'm quite safe. I've never touched one diseased body.

2ND CITIZEN. You're very lucky not to be risking your life for other people. But other people are risking theirs for you. Still, don't be too pleased with yourself, it's almost impossible to know who is in good health and who

38

is not. You can see people full of life, apparently healthy enough, in the pink of condition, who an hour later will be dead.

1ST CITIZEN. If I've escaped up till now, I'll escape all right in the time to come. I'm not a selfish man, so long as no-one asks too much of me. In normal circumstances I don't mind helping out. Now we're living in exceptional times, and we have a right, a duty to be cautious and suspicious. At serious moments like these we have a right and a duty to be provisionally selfish.

2ND CITIZEN. I suppose that's one way of looking at things.

1ST CITIZEN. I'm quite safe. I've a flair for staying out of trouble. I've never been with people who present the slightest threat. I never see doctors or nurses. I avoid undertakers' mutes, and I buy my food only in very high-class grocers. It's better to fork out a few more pence than to feel oneself in danger. My life is worth no less than other people's.

2ND CITIZEN. The day before yesterday it was reported you were seen in the 'Stuffed Turkey'. Were you not in one of their dining-rooms at a table with Monsieur Daniel?

1ST CITIZEN. What of it? That gentleman is a friend of mine and we were talking business. He's a plump, fine-looking man. He takes the same precautions as I do. There was no-one in our private cubicle likely to infect us.

2ND CITIZEN. I see.

1ST CITIZEN. Why do you say: 'I see?'

2ND CITIZEN. I say: 'I see' because I say: 'I see'. Did I say: 'I see?' Don't come near me.

1ST CITIZEN. You're not going to tell me...

2ND CITIZEN. I've nothing to tell you.

1ST CITIZEN. Tell me what you mean when you say you've nothing to tell me.

2ND CITIZEN. Don't come near me I say! And don't make me repeat it.

1ST CITIZEN. That gentleman, the friend I was dining with, is he ill? Tell me, is he ill?

2ND CITIZEN. No. He's not ill. He's not ill any more.

1ST CITIZEN. He recovered so soon?

2ND CITIZEN. Not that either. He's dead.

1st CITIZEN. Perhaps he died of a heart attack. Perhaps he died accidentally? Did he fall? Was he murdered?

2ND CITIZEN. If you want the truth, he died of the disease.

1ST CITIZEN. Then I'm going to die too.

2ND CITIZEN. For the third time I tell you that's no reason to come near me. If you take another step, I'll draw my pistol.

1ST CITIZEN. So I'm dead then! Unless there's a miracle. I'm as good as dead. (A NURSE passes) Nurse! I'm afraid I may have been contaminated. Come here! (He opens his jacket and unbuttons his shirt)

NURSE. (examining the 1ST CITIZEN's chest) Oh, it's too late, too late now! No medicine can help you now. (She moves away from him)

1ST CITIZEN. (running off to the Left and shouting) I'm a dead man, I'm a dead man!

(The 2ND CITIZEN runs after the 1ST CITIZEN and fires at him. The NURSE runs after the 2ND CITIZEN as he runs after the 1ST CITIZEN and shouts)

NURSE. And you're a dead man too! And I'm a dead woman!

PRISON SCENE

(1ST PRISONER, 2ND PRISONER, JAILER)

1ST PRISONER. That's two of the bars sawn through. All you have to do is to give a little shove and bob's your uncle. We can escape through the window.

2ND PRISONER. To fall into the moat. There's water in it.

1ST PRISONER. You knew that before. But you know how to swim. Anyway, I've told you that in five minutes we'll be on dry land. Over in that sunny field. And after, there are gardens, and then streets and then shops, the butcher's and the baker's, the wine merchant's and the greengrocer's.

2ND PRISONER. Look out! Hide the file, someone's coming. It's our jailer.

(Enter the JAILER)

JAILER. The gates are wide open for you. The door I've just come through has not been closed again, and none of the other doors have been shut. I know you want to escape through the window, and I know you have a file. It's not worth going to all that trouble now. We're all in trouble, a new warder, more dangerous than we were.

1ST PRISONER. I'm not scared of unemployment. I'm not afraid of fire or water.

JAILER. That's not the point in dispute any more.

1ST PRISONER. You won't make me back down. You may be able to put _him_ off. (Indicating the 2ND PRISONER) But I'm not your man. Every now and again _he_ has his doubts.

JAILER. The warders who are at the gates are dead.

2ND PRISONER. How's that? What happened to them? Why didn't you send for more warders?

JAILER. Oh, we did, they have been replaced. By invisible warders.

1ST PRISONER. You're joking.

JAILER. That is not one of my habits. A sickness is raging through the town. Everywhere within the city walls, up to the very gates, which are closed, guarded by soldiers who may die at any moment. Even if they did, the gates would not be opened again, for there are guards outside the city to prevent you from leaving.

1ST PRISONER. Within the city walls is good enough for me.

2ND PRISONER. And for me.

JAILER. The guards outside don't have the disease, at least they haven't yet. They don't want to catch it, that's why they won't let you leave. They're afraid of being contaminated. Inside the city almost everyone is infected. Those who haven't caught it yet probably will do soon.

2ND PRISONER. What disease?

JAILER. A disease that kills. This epidemic allows no hope. People are lying on the pavements, in the middle of the roadway, in locked apartments, in the churches and the chapels. We can't even collect them now. Even the undertaker's mutes are threatened, and they swore not to fall ill. Imagine, they were actually under oath. So we really thought they were immunised. Dogs and cats, horses and rats, are lying there too beside the human corpses. Since Monday, 30,000 new bodies have been counted, men, women and beasts. Twice as many as last week, three times as many as the week before.

2ND PRISONER. It's not possible.

1ST PRISONER. You're lying, you're trying to frighten me. Yes, that's it, it must be a lie put out by the Town Council!

JAILER. Go and see. And soon you'll see and hear no
more. You'll feel nothing more. The Prison Governor
died because he went out, because he went out every
evening to see his wife and children. He was infected by
his family, he died surrounded by his dear ones, all
dead. My colleagues died too for the same reason.
Yesterday a tram set off from one side of the town to
the other, full of passengers. They all died during the
journey. When it reached its destination, they counted
87 dead, 88 with the conductor.

2ND PRISONER. No-one's obliged to take a tram.

JAILER. Pedestrians aren't any safer. Bodies of the dead
and dying fall on them from the windows. But I'm a
bachelor, I've no relations. I never leave the prison. In
prison there's no danger. Look how thick the walls
are. Nothing can get in. Not even microbes. Of course,
you may feel you're in prison here, but there's no
danger. You can consider yourselves home and dry.
The real prison, that's outside. You choose between
prison or death.

1ST PRISONER. It's not true. It can't be true!

JAILER. Go on out then, if you like.

1ST PRISONER. It's a trap.

JAILER. But I tell you I'm leaving the door open for you,
try it! I tell you all the doors are open. (He goes out)

2ND PRISONER. (to the 1ST) What do you think you'll do?

1ST PRISONER. He's a liar. He's cunning.

2ND PRISONER. He's not lying.

1ST PRISONER. What do you know about it? Have you any
proof?

2ND PRISONER. Last night I dreamt everyone was dying,
it was a nightmare and I saw mountains of the dead.
They were piled up so high they towered over six-storey

houses. You see, he did leave the door open.

1ST PRISONER. It's because you haven't the guts to escape. You're chicken.

2ND PRISONER. The door's open all right, look!

1ST PRISONER. Don't tell me you believe in dreams.

2ND PRISONER. There's truth in dreams. What one doesn't dare imagine by day, dreams reveal to you by night.

1ST PRISONER. You dream to suit yourself. A dream shows you what you're too scared of. It gives you a false alibi. It's an excuse for cowardice.

2ND PRISONER. If the door's open, it's because there's no more need for warders. I'd rather end my days in prison, at a ripe old age.

1ST PRISONER. I'll go on my own. But I don't trust warders. They must be guarding the other doors. He lied to us. There must be some warders around, alive and kicking, bursting with health. You can never trust a warder. I must go. The Party needs me. I've got a mission, I've got my duty to others. Long live freedom. You can follow me if you like. I'll go through the window. I don't trust doors. Goodbye.

(He can be seen jumping through the window, after tearing out the two bars, which he throws to the ground)

2ND PRISONER. (climbing on the stool to look through the window) He won't get far.

VOICE OF THE 1ST PRISONER. The rats are biting me. I'm in pain all over. I can't swim any more. I'm sinking! Help!

2ND PRISONER. (stepping down off the stool to face the public) Already a bloated corpse is floating on the water.

JAILER. (returning) Now you see that I told the truth.

44

2ND PRISONER. I always believed you. (The JAILER takes out his pistol. Terrified) I always believed you. I always believed you. I tell you I always believed you. You're not going to kill me!

(The JAILER fires on the PRISONER, who falls. Then, for no apparent reason, he takes a rope with a running noose from his pocket and hangs himself. The BLACK MONK crosses the stage, checks that the PRISONER's pulse has stopped, verifies the strength of the hanged man's rope and goes out)

(Street scene. JACQUES, EMILE, PIERRE. PIERRE enters from the Left, the two others from the Right)

PIERRE. How are you?

JACQUES. How are you?

EMILE. How are you?

PIERRE. I've had migraine. It's much better now. I suppose recent events have made too great an impression on me. You know about it?

EMILE. What events?

JACQUES. What events? You're referring to...

PIERRE. The disease. In the city. The epidemic that's raging through the slums.

EMILE. It's only in the slums that it's raging, we're quite safe here. Of course in the slums, you know, ignorance ...

JACQUES. Lack of hygiene...

EMILE. Vice...and poverty.

JACQUES. Yes, there's the poverty too, the squalor. It's a filthy thing, squalor.

EMILE. Poverty is a vice. They're poor because they want to be, the dregs. Drunk and idle, they just let themselves go. The misery of squalor is the mother of all vice.

JACQUES. You could also say that vice is the father of all misery.

PIERRE. You think it won't reach us here?

EMILE. I don't think so. We're not down-and-out.

JACQUES. (to PIERRE) You know Alexander's dead.

PIERRE. How, when, why? He was getting better. He was convalescent.

EMILE. He's dead. But not from the epidemic. The epidemic doesn't get inside the hospitals.

JACQUES. Except perhaps those in the slums. And yet... After all, they are our doctors, the doctors from the nice districts, who run these other hospitals and keep an eye on things... They wouldn't let the epidemic inside.

PIERRE. What did he die of?

JACQUES. It was rather unexpected, anyway not the epidemic. He didn't show any of the signs.

EMILE. He died because he wanted to die.

JACQUES. He did it on purpose.

EMILE. A way of showing off. A showman to the last.

JACQUES. He was getting over his illness. A convalescence that took the wrong turning.

PIERRE. It's most upsetting, I needed him. Friends are the people you need, it takes time, and luck, to replace them. When my wife gets to hear...

46

EMILE. (to PIERRE) Is that your headache back again?

JACQUES. It's the shock. It's understandable. You look rather tired.

EMILE. You've gone pale. No, not pale now, your colour's back in your cheeks.

PIERRE. I've no more migraine at all. One has to get over things. That's what living is: getting life over. Anyway, I feel better, I feel much better. (He falls)

EMILE. What's the matter with him?

JACQUES. What's the matter with him?

EMILE. Come on, old chap, stand up, wake up!

JACQUES. Heart failure.

EMILE. Perhaps he's just fainted.

JACQUES. No, he's dead.

EMILE. What can have come over him? He was feeling better.

STREET SCENE

A PASSER-BY. (to his COMPANION) When I left my friends' house, there were two of them. I went out to fetch the paper and came back. Climbed the stairs and then, well, I opened the door and saw eleven bodies stretched out.

COMPANION. How did they multiply themselves like that?

PASSER-BY. What we need to know, what we've got to establish, is this: did they multiply themselves while they were alive, or later? Anyway, it all took just five minutes.

COMPANION. Perhaps it was done by computer.

47

(The stage is divided into two and the two following
scenes are to be played simultaneously.

On the side of the stage that is audience Left, there is
a window at the rear, a door on the Left and a bed on
the Right, against the wall, real or imaginary, which
separates the two sides of the stage.

On the other side of the stage there is also a bed against
the wall, a window at the rear and a door on the Right.

There is also a chair in each of the two rooms thus
formed.

The first of the two simultaneous scenes, Scene A,
takes place in the room audience Left. There is a knock
on the door. The first woman, JEANNE, will already
have been seen rising painfully from her chair, obviously
a prey to anxiety. She rushes to open the door.

Enter a man, JEAN)

JEANNE. How did you manage?

JEAN. In the dark I slipped between the sentinels guarding
the town. Coming through the gates and along the
avenue, I nearly got caught several times by the patrols.

JEANNE. You would have been much safer down in the
country. But I'm happy to see you. I'd stopped hoping. I
didn't want you to be here, but I like you being here.

JEAN. Well, here I am. The children stayed behind, with
your family. There's nothing to fear for them. They're all
right.

JEANNE. What's going to become of us?

JEAN. Perhaps God knows. Do you know that monk
standing in front of our house?

JEANNE. Do you think it will ever end?

JEAN. Perhaps. It's hardly safe to go out. The silence

48

there is in the street! There's a shop open at the
corner. I'll go and fetch some food.

JEANNE. There's no hurry, darling. Come and sit next
to me.

(She takes him by the hand. They go and sit on the bed
next to each other. He holds her by the shoulders)

What was the weather like?

JEAN. Nice and fresh. There's the sea, and the sea wind
healing everything. You're a bundle of nerves.

JEANNE. Here it's been terribly hot. And the foul air...

JEAN. You're too scared. You mustn't be scared. We're
together, aren't we? It may be nothing will happen to us.

JEANNE. The people on the ground floor are dead. They
took the bodies away. The people on the floor above have
fled. No-one knows where.

JEAN. They must be wandering through the streets. They'll
be asked for their papers. They'll be brought back. Or
they'll be kept in isolation.

JEANNE. What have we all done, for it to be like this?

JEAN. Nothing. We've done nothing. It's all like this for
nothing. There is no reason. At least, if it were a
punishment...

JEANNE. Perhaps it is a punishment.

JEAN. Of course. If it was, we'd be easier in our minds.
But there's been nothing. We've done nothing. This
scourge is without a cause.

JEANNE. We were happy.

JEAN. And we didn't know.

JEANNE. I can't help being scared.

(Pause. JEAN stands up)

If you hadn't come, I'd have gone mad.

JEAN. Now be a good girl and calm down.

JEANNE. No. I can't stay here. Let's go out for a while.

JEAN. Have a little rest. You're quite pale.

JEANNE. I'm pale?

JEAN. It's nothing, it's nervous. Lie down for a moment.
(He helps her to stretch herself out) There, that's it.
I'm near you. Give me your hand. Your hand is hot
and moist.

JEANNE. I have a headache.

JEAN. Do you want me to open the window?

JEANNE. Who knows what may come in from the street?

JEAN. And you wanted to go out! How your forehead
burns! (He undoes her blouse) Oh God!

JEANNE. (her hand flying to her throat) I'm swollen,
aren't I? Look, the palms of my hands are red! I've
a pain in my stomach. I feel weak. I've got pains everywhere.

JEAN. I'll look after you! I'll take care of you!

JEANNE. That bottle!

JEAN. (taking a little bottle from his pocket) Take a deep
breath.

JEANNE. I can't.

JEAN. Take a deep breath.

JEANNE. I can't feel anything. Absolutely nothing.

JEAN. Make an effort, my darling. I'm beside you, close beside you.

JEANNE. I can hardly see you. It's like through a mist.

JEAN. There's no mist in the house.

JEANNE. I feel so ill and I'm frightened.

JEAN. It's nothing, my darling. It's nothing.

JEANNE. I can only just hear your words.

JEAN. (shouting) Don't feel frightened, that's all! These salts will cure you. I'll take you in my arms and never leave you.

JEANNE. Speak to me.

JEAN. I'll hold you tight in my arms. I have you and I'll keep you. Nothing can snatch you away from me. I'll not leave you.

JEANNE. Are you near me? I can't see you. I can't hear you. Are you holding me in your arms? I can't feel you.

JEAN. Don't go away, please, please! Stay with me. I came back for you. Don't leave me.

JEANNE. I feel so ill. Are you there? I waited for you. I was hoping for you. Why didn't you come? I'm all alone.

JEAN. But I'm here, my darling. Listen to me. Look at me. Can't you feel me? Speak to me! Speak!

(She utters a sigh and dies)

(Folding her in his arms) I'll stay close to you, I won't go away. Till the end of time, I'll be here.

(Scene B. Simultaneous with Scene A. This scene takes place on the stage audience Right. There is a knock at

(the door. We will already have seen the woman,
LUCIENNE, rise painfully from her chair. She rushes
to open the door. Enter a man, PIERRE)

LUCIENNE. How did you manage?

PIERRE. In the dark I slipped between the sentinels
guarding the town. Coming through the gates and along
the avenue, I nearly got caught several times by the
patrols.

LUCIENNE. You would have been much safer down in the
country. But I'm happy to see you. I'd stopped hoping.
I didn't want you to be here, but I like you being here.

PIERRE. Well, here I am. The children stayed behind with
your family. There's nothing to fear for them. They're
all right.

LUCIENNE. What's going to become of us?

PIERRE. Perhaps God knows. Do you know that monk
standing in front of our house?

LUCIENNE. Do you think it will ever end?

PIERRE. Perhaps. It's hardly safe to go out. The silence
there in the street! There's a shop open at the corner.
I'll go and fetch some food.

(Stage directions: the dialogue in Scene B alternates with
the dialogue of Scene A until the moment when, towards
the end of the scene, it changes. That moment will be
indicated. So, when JEANNE says: 'How did you
manage?', LUCIENNE says to PIERRE: 'How did you
manage?', then JEAN's second speech: 'In the dark,
etc.', is followed by PIERRE's speech: 'In the dark,
etc.', and so until the moment indicated)

LUCIENNE. There's no hurry, darling. Come and sit next
to me.

(She takes him by the hand. They go and sit on the bed
next to each other. He holds her by the shoulders)

What was the weather like?

PIERRE. Nice and fresh. There's the sea, and the sea wind healing everything. You're a bundle of nerves.

LUCIENNE. Here it's been terribly hot. And the foul air...

PIERRE. You're too scared. You mustn't be scared. We're together, aren't we? It may be nothing will happen to us.

LUCIENNE. The people on the ground floor are dead. They took the bodies away. The people on the floor above have fled. No-one knows where.

PIERRE. They must be wandering through the streets. They'll be asked for their papers. They'll be brought back. Or they'll be kept in isolation.

LUCIENNE. What have we all done, for it to be like this?

PIERRE. Nothing. We've done nothing. It's all like this for nothing. There is no reason. At least, if it were a punishment...

LUCIENNE. Perhaps it is a punishment.

PIERRE. Of course. If it was, we'd be easier in our minds. But there's been nothing. We've done nothing. This scourge is without a cause.

LUCIENNE. We were happy.

PIERRE. And we didn't know.

LUCIENNE. I can't help being scared.

(Pause. PIERRE stands up. Change from Scene A)

PIERRE. If I hadn't come, I'd have gone mad.

LUCIENNE. Now you be a good boy and keep calm.

PIERRE. No. I can't stay here. Let's go out for a while.

53

LUCIENNE. Have a little rest. You're quite pale.

PIERRE. I'm pale?

LUCIENNE. It's nothing, it's nervous. Lie down for a
moment.

(She helps him to stretch himself out)

There, that's it. I'm near you. Give me your hand.
Your hand is hot and moist.

PIERRE. I have a headache.

LUCIENNE. Do you want me to open the window?

PIERRE. Who knows what may come in from the street?

LUCIENNE. And you wanted to go out! How your forehead
burns! Oh God!

PIERRE. Oh God!

LUCIENNE. You seem to be swelling! Look, the palms of
your hands are red!

PIERRE. I've a pain in my stomach. I feel weak. I've got
pains everywhere.

LUCIENNE. How can I help you? What can I do?

PIERRE. That bottle! Give me that bottle!

LUCIENNE. My God, it's too late. He's got the sickness
already.

PIERRE. I'd like to take a deep breath, but I can't.

LUCIENNE. I'm so frightened, my darling.

PIERRE. I can't feel anything.

LUCIENNE. Make an effort. I'm here. (She is panic-
stricken)

54

PIERRE. I can hardly see you. It's like through a mist.

LUCIENNE. There's no mist in the house.

PIERRE. I feel so ill.

LUCIENNE. It's nothing, my darling. I'm sure it's nothing.

PIERRE. I can hardly hear your words.

LUCIENNE. (shouting) Help me! There's no-one.

PIERRE. Speak to me.

LUCIENNE. (already making slowly for the door) What am I going to do? Poor woman! With a dying man on her hands! Everyone's abandoned us!

PIERRE. Are you near me? I can't see you. I can't hear you. Are you holding me in your arms? I can't feel you.

(LUCIENNE utters a cry and opens the door)

Don't go away, please, please! I came here for you. Don't leave me. I feel so ill.

LUCIENNE. And I was waiting for him. And I thought we were going to go away together, to safety together. (She goes out while she says this)

PIERRE. I feel so ill. Are you here? Are you still here? You're not going to leave me, not going to desert me! I know you're here, my darling. I can see you. I can hear you. I can feel you. Speak a little louder! I'm not alone.

CURTAIN. END OF SCENE.

(The stage is divided in two. Two simultaneous scenes.

On one side of the stage, audience Left, a divan, a dressing table, a window to the rear and a chair.

On the other side of the stage, audience Right, a bed.
This is a room in an inn. On the Left-hand side, the
MOTHER, the DAUGHTER and the MAID. The
DAUGHTER is in front of the dressing table)

MOTHER. Make yourself look nice, daughter. Put your
ear-rings on. And your necklace. We're going to the
forbidden ball.

(On the Right-hand side of the stage, the TRAVELLER,
looking harassed, comes in followed by a SERVING-
GIRL from the inn)

SERVING-GIRL. Our inn has a good reputation, sir. You can
rest assured. No bugs here.

(From the left-hand scene)

MAID. Here's your best perfume, Miss.

MOTHER. (to her DAUGHTER) Come on now, make
yourself beautiful! You've got to look right for your
fiancé. Make yourself specially beautiful!

DAUGHTER. Yes, mother. I'll try.

(From the right-hand scene)

SERVING-GIRL. (to the TRAVELLER) A man in black has
just gone past again. Do you know him?

(From the left-hand scene)

MOTHER. Forget all your worries. You must enjoy
yourself, you're young. We all have friends who are
dead. We haven't the time to weep for them.

MAID. That man in black has just walked along the street
again, Madam.

(From the Right)

TRAVELLER. Bring me a pint of beer, please.

SERVING-GIRL. Our beer is first-rate. Very good for you.

(She goes out. The TRAVELLER stretches out on the
bed. Then be begins to moan. He stiffens up, then
falls from the bed. Climbs back again with difficulty.
He enters his last agony. Death rattle and death.
Meanwhile, on the Left-hand side of the stage, the
DAUGHTER will have the same symptoms of the disease,
and the following takes place)

DAUGHTER. Oh God! Always that man in black. What does
it mean?

MOTHER. Oh, don't worry about it.

DAUGHTER. Ever since this morning he's been walking
backwards and forwards beneath our window.

MOTHER. He's a monk, just a poor monk. (To the MAID)
Don't frighten her so, what's the matter with you?

MAID. He's not a good omen.

MOTHER. He's going to visit the sick, to cheer them up
and encourage them. He's a brave man. (To the
DAUGHTER) Now you just make yourself beautiful!
Think of all the happy things, there's so much to think
of. The spring and the lakes and the fields and the
flowers...

DAUGHTER. Do you like the necklace, mother? Somehow
I don't feel like wearing it.

MOTHER. The scourge will spare us, I'm sure it will.

MAID. (to the DAUGHTER) Would you like a different
perfume? Here are your rings. And your powder.

(The DAUGHTER puts the rings on her fingers and the
powder on her face)

MOTHER. You can put some rouge on your face and redden
your lips.

DAUGHTER. I'm pale, aren't I?

MAID. There are some guards outside the door of the house opposite.

MOTHER. They're not there for us. Not there for us.

MAID. May Heaven hear your words, Madam.

DAUGHTER. I feel tired. So tired. I don't feel like doing anything.

MOTHER. Come along, you must pull yourself together. Stir yourself, darling. Would you like me to help you dress?

DAUGHTER. I have a headache.

(The DAUGHTER gets up and staggers)

MAID. (to the DAUGHTER) What's the matter, Miss?

MOTHER. Nothing, I tell you. Nothing wrong with her at all. A touch of migraine, I expect. And that's because she's shy, she doesn't like social occasions. She's a bit upset, a touch of nerves. (To the DAUGHTER) Come on, I'll help you dress, and make you look really nice.

DAUGHTER. I think I'd rather... I'd like to lie down for a moment.

MOTHER. Have a rest then, if you like. Not too long though, we've got to leave in a few minutes.

(The DAUGHTER nearly falls. Her MOTHER rushes to her)

(To the MAID) Help me! A little cold water. (To the DAUGHTER) It's just a little turn.

(The MOTHER and the MAID help the DAUGHTER to lie down on the divan)

DAUGHTER. Mother, I feel very ill.

58

MAID. She's gone all white.

MOTHER. How do you feel? Where do you feel the pain?

DAUGHTER. My head. My eyes. My throat. My stomach. I'm cold. I'm too hot. I'm stifling.

MAID. Her forehead is burning. And her hands are as cold as ice.

(The MOTHER undoes the DAUGHTER's blouse)

But look, she's all red! Purple. The palms of her hands are turning black. Better not touch her.

MOTHER. It's not that. It can't be that.

MAID. (shouting) She's got the scourge.

MOTHER. (throwing herself over her DAUGHTER) Don't be frightened, darling! I'll take care of you. It's nothing. You'll get better.

MAID. She's got the scourge.

MOTHER. Be quiet! It's just a bad turn, I tell you.

DAUGHTER. It hurts.

MAID. God has struck at us.

(On the right-hand side of the stage)

SERVING-GIRL. (as she arrives) Here is your beer, sir. Look, he's dead! He died here, in the inn.

(On the left-hand side of the stage)

MAID. Help! Help!

(She rushes through the door in the dividing wall and crosses the TRAVELLER's bedroom, while the SERVING-GIRL cries out 'He's dead, he's dead!' The latter throws the beer to the ground and goes out,

59

colliding with the MAID, so that they both rush out of the TRAVELLER's bedroom together, getting in each other's way, and shouting: 'Help, friends! Help!' On the Left side of the stage the MOTHER is distraught, clasping her DAUGHTER's body to her)

MOTHER. We were so happy. You had everything, you had everything, alas! (She utters the most terrible cries and runs to the window, then comes back to her DAUGHTER) Alas, woe is me! Help! Help!

(She throws herself on her DAUGHTER's bed, then goes to the window and comes back to her DAUGHTER on the bed, where she throws herself down)

Help me! Have pity!

(From the Left enter the BLACK MONK, who stands quite still, without a word)

NIGHT SCENE

(The stage is dark. At the rear, at a level mid-way between the floor and the flies, there are five lighted windows, or windows which will perhaps light up one after the other.

In the darkness the first thing one sees is a lantern being lit. One can just glimpse the person carrying the lantern. It is the Black-robed MONK, who crosses the stage from Right to Left. As soon as he has gone out, we can hear the shrill scream of a WOMAN, very drawn out. Then, after two seconds of silence, one can see the first window on the Right - by that I mean on the Audience Left - which lights up. A WOMAN appears there, with loose flowing hair, shouting)

1ST WOMAN. Death! Death! Death! Help!

(A second window lights up. TWO WOMEN and a very YOUNG MAN are moving about in desperate agitation. They appear and disappear as in a Punch and Judy show)

(At the first window) Death! Help! My dear brothers, help me!

2ND WOMAN. (at the 2nd window) Help! Come and help us!

YOUNG MAN. (at the 2nd window) Help us! Our father has hanged himself!

(The third window lights up. An OLD MAN appears and a 2ND MAN)

1ST WOMAN. Help! Don't leave me! A priest! A doctor!

3RD WOMAN. (at the 2nd window) A doctor! He can still be brought back to life! My father-in-law has hanged himself!

YOUNG MAN. My father has hanged himself! Doctor! Fire Brigade!

(At the 3rd window you can see the OLD MAN, who without uttering a sound, takes a revolver from his pocket, very slowly. At the 2nd window, ONE of the WOMEN disappears, then the YOUNG MAN, while the 3RD WOMAN cries for help)

3RD WOMAN. Doctor! Doctor! Doctor!

1ST WOMAN. (at the 1st window) Death! Come and help us!

(At the 2nd window the 3RD WOMAN is seen to disappear, while the YOUNG MAN and 2ND WOMAN reappear. The 2ND WOMAN and the YOUNG MAN reappear at the 2nd window while the 3RD WOMAN disappears with much gesticulation. All of them give the impression of being puppets)

YOUNG MAN. Help us! You bastards! You cowards!

(A 4th window lights up, the grey head and bent shoulders of an ELDERLY WOMAN can be seen, standing with her back to the window, who shouts out in terror in the direction of a character who will be seen appearing in a moment)

4TH WOMAN. Please, please, I implore you, no!

(At the 3rd window the OLD MAN can be seen raising
his revolver to his temple. At the 1st window the 1ST
WOMAN sobs in despair, her hair in disorder, her arms
lifted to Heaven. At the 2nd window the YOUNG MAN and
the YOUNG WOMAN disappear, while the 3RD WOMAN
appears)

3RD WOMAN. With oxygen perhaps we could revive him!
Help! Oh, quick!

4TH WOMAN. (still with her back to the window) Help!

1ST WOMAN. Help!

2ND WOMAN. (who reappears at the window while the 3RD
WOMAN disappears) Help!

YOUNG MAN. (reappearing) Help!

(At the 3rd window one can now see the OLD MAN
holding the pistol to his head)

OLD MAN. A country of imbeciles! A city of cretins!

(At the 4th window, next to the OLD MAN, a NURSE
can be seen making for the latter, with her hands held
out threateningly, as if to strangle her)

NURSE. Old witch!

4TH WOMAN. (trying to break away) I won't! I won't!
Help!

1ST WOMAN. (at the 1st window)   )
2ND & 3RD WOMEN.   ) Help! Help!
4TH WOMAN.   )

YOUNG MAN. Help my father!

(The 5th window lights up and a MAN appears dressed

62

in his pyjamas. He seems to have just got out of bed)

3RD MAN. No-one can get any sleep! Shut up!

NURSE. It's all over for you. I'll have your money.

4TH WOMAN. I was leaving it to the poor.

1ST WOMAN. Help!

2ND & 3RD WOMEN. Help!

NURSE. (to the 4TH WOMAN) Liar! Old witch!

(She closes in on the 4TH WOMAN, who screams)

3RD MAN. (at the 5th window) Be quiet and think of others for once!

(The YOUNG MAN disappears again for a moment from the 2nd window)

NURSE. (rushing at the 4TH WOMAN) Pestilence!

1ST & 2ND WOMEN. Who will hear us! Come and help us!

(The NURSE takes the 4TH WOMAN by the throat)

4TH WOMAN. No-o-o-o! (She utters a terrible cry and falls)

YOUNG MAN. (reappearing at the 2nd window and holding the TWO WOMEN round the shoulders) Our father is dead.

3RD MAN. (at the 5th window) I've got to work tomorrow morning!

(TWO POLICEMEN arrive, each carrying a machine-gun)

1ST POLICEMAN. No-one to leave this house, or I fire! (He takes aim)

63

3RD MAN. (at the 5th window) Shut up!

2ND POLICEMAN. They'll not come out, dead or alive!
   (The 4TH WOMAN falls with a scream inside the house)

OLD MAN. Idiot! (He fires and falls through the window
   into the street)

1ST WOMAN. Death! (She throws herself through the
   window and falls into the street)

2ND & 3RD WOMEN & YOUNG MAN. Help!

3RD MAN. (clasping his hands to his ears) Shut up! I can't
   stand this ear-splitting row!

1ST POLICEMAN. (to the 2ND, indicating the bodies lying
   in the street) They managed to get out, anyway!

2ND POLICEMAN. (while the three other characters are
   shouting for help and the 3RD MAN is demanding silence)
   We'd better go and finish off the others! We don't want
   no nonsense!

   (Stage directions: the 2ND and 3RD WOMEN and the
   YOUNG MAN could still go on gesticulating at
   their window, but they might just as well, with no
   apparent justification, each appear at one of the last
   three windows, still jerking their arms about like
   puppets)

                      END OF SCENE

   (Author's indications: If this scene is used, if will appear
   as the sequel to the preceding scene, with no lowering of
   the curtain. The curtain will be lowered at the end of
   this scene.

   Enter an OFFICER with two other POLICEMEN)

OFFICER. (to the 1ST and 2ND POLICEMEN, who, after one
   has heard shouts and shots from inside the houses,
   followed by a silence, come out of the house, putting their
   pistols back in their holsters) Your report.

1ST POLICEMAN. We did what had to be done, sir.

2ND POLICEMAN. All according to orders. (He points in the direction of the windows) May God have mercy on their souls!

OFFICER. (to TWO OTHER POLICEMEN, who have just arrived) You can take over from the other wardens. Dawn is breaking. You will be relieved at midday. Watch and keep your eyes open. Your instructions are the same. No-one is to enter the infected houses you are guarding. Or leave. In exceptional cases and with the full authorisation of the Chief of Police, certain people may be allowed to go into these houses, but they must never come out again. Any infraction of this law is punishable by death. You fire point blank at any person who tries to break this emergency law. Equally subject to the death penalty, is any one of you who has proved himself unable to prevent anyone leaving these houses. When asked by the people locked inside, you may give them food and drink. You half-open the door and throw the provisions into the hall. Then you lock the doors again and under no pretext whatsoever will you leave your post.

(They remain at attention. The OFFICER turns towards the 1ST TWO POLICEMEN)

Inspection.

(The 1ST & 2ND POLICEMEN show their hands and undo the collars of their tunics. The OFFICER carefully inspects the hands, faces and throats of each of his men. After inspecting the 2ND POLICEMAN, he exclaims)

The signs...

(The 2ND POLICEMAN tries to escape. The others surround him and try to make him enter a house with a red cross on the door. The 2ND POLICEMAN is still trying to escape. The three other POLICEMEN kill him)

OFFICER. I'll send for another warden at once. And I'll ask for a death cart to take him away. Don't touch him. Who knifed this man? (The 1ST POLICEMAN steps forward)

1ST POLICEMAN. I did.

(The 3RD POLICEMAN steps forward)

3RD POLICEMAN. I did.

OFFICER. Throw away those knives. They touched him.
You will have others. (Indicating the other bodies
lying over the stage) The car can take all that away too.

STREET SCENE 1

(On the Right side of the stage a POLITICIAN on a
platform is haranguing the crowd, that is to say THREE
ACTORS: and over the heads of these ACTORS the
Audience. At the back, a shop selling ladies' hats,
dresses and fancy goods)

ORATOR. Dear fellow citizens, I have brought you here
together to speak to you of the future of our city. I have
broken the regulations which forbade such public
meetings, and large numbers of you have arrived under
the nose and in the teeth of our present rulers. They
want to shut us up in our homes and in our misery. Under
the pretext of a disease that is raging amongst us - and
all pretexts are good for our rulers - under the pretext
of protecting us against the scourge, we have been
immobilised, prevented from acting, paralysed,
dominated and destroyed. This sickness kills as many
inside their houses as out. Even more inside the houses,
where the air is fetid, and it is in fetid air that the
scourge develops best. In the open air, it has less
potency. Not more, anyway. It's bad policy to be
confined, bad for us, but for our rulers the tactics are
diabolical. They want to restrain us from a healthy
revolt, they want to restrain us from formulating our
rightful grievances, they want to restrain us from forming
groups, they want to isolate us to make us powerless,
an easier prey to the scourge. I even wonder if this
disease that they treat as so mysterious is not of their
own invention. And why do they call it mysterious? In

order to conceal its origins, its basic causes. That is
why we are here, to de-mystify this mystery. In
whose interest is it that this disease should continue? In
ours? It can hardly be ours, for we die of it. Our death
is a matter of politics. We are playing our oppressors'
game, for we are their playthings. Do you know the
statistics? 190,000 citizens have died for no apparent
cause in these recent weeks, since the scourge has been
raging, 190,000, perhaps even 200,000 by now, as our
statistics are two days old, and that means almost a
quarter of the population. Some 40 to 60,000, according
to our calculations, are lying at death's door in the
hospitals, for they're being helped to die rather than to
survive. 60,000 others are lying in their houses with
the undertakers ready for action at their doors. If the
undertakers are ready for action, who alerted them?
Our rulers. Which means that's what they're expecting,
they're prepared for it, planned it perhaps. 200,000
dead and 100,000 sick or dying, that makes nearly a
third of the population already disposed of. How many City
Councillors have we? The Council consists of twenty-
one people. Out of these twenty-one, four are no longer
in the precincts of our town. They were on holiday at the
time when the scourge appeared and the gates were
closed. We are told that they were unable to enter. We
are not so green. Foreseeing what was to come, they
sought safety, for they knew what was coming. Four
Councillors out of twenty-one, that makes almost a
fifth of their total number. You will tell me that there
were ordinary citizens too, outside the city on holiday.
There are indeed a few outside the city. But only one-
twentieth of the total population. Everyone couldn't be
prevented from leaving. That would have been clumsy.
However, the fact that one-fifth of our administrators are
not here, and only one-twentieth of the administered
is brilliant proof of how machiavellically our affairs
have been jerry-mandered. Out of seventeen Councillors
on duty in the city, only three are dead. Proportionally to
the percentage of deaths in the city, this is an insignificant
figure. And out of the three Councillors who died one
supported our legitimate claims. He was an enemy of
the President of the Council and a friend of the people.
The other two were indeterminate characters,
supporters of the President of the Council, but half-

hearted and only partially committed. You will object
that these three Councillors were not actually
assassinated by order of the rest? Obviously. However,
even while admitting your objection, may I draw your
attention to the fact that it is not the cause of the death
of these three Councillors which is in question, not the
rational cause. But what is clear is the significance of
the fact that these three victims were actually or
potentially opposed to the regime. By the same token, if
it is by chance that the four Councillors happened to be
on holiday - and it is by no means sure as I told you just
now that they were on holiday by chance - this fact is
equally significant, as it is due to objective chance. But
we still have seventeen administratively alive administrators left. If things go on at this rate, they will soon
represent one-tenth of the total population of our city:
easy enough to govern such a city, when its strength
is so effectively reduced. Those who are not dead will
be entirely in their hands, tied both hand and foot.

1ST CHARACTER. (out of the THREE surrounding the
ORATOR) It's nobody's fault.

ORATOR. I don't say it is. Not a 100%. But once
again, it is not the cause of the disease but its significance
that we should be considering. Who profits from all these
deaths? We must seek out those who profit by it.

2ND CHARACTER. No-one profits by it. They burn all the
belongings of the dead.

ORATOR. And the houses? Are their houses burnt too?
And their bank accounts, do they disappear with the dead?

3RD CHARACTER. They belong to their heirs. Or else to
the heirs of their heirs, or to the heirs of the heirs of
their heirs.

ORATOR. All that's needed is a law by which they pass to
their survivors. And, dear fellow citizens, they certainly
won't be all of us here, if we go on not taking action. The
privileged ones will be chosen by objective chance, but
already picked out by our infamous rulers.

1ST CHARACTER. Let's take action!

2ND CHARACTER. What shall we do?

3RD CHARACTER. Tell us what we should do.

ORATOR. Revolt. Activism. Violence. I do not promise
that the scourge will disappear, but I promise that its
meaning will be changed. Let us kill the undertakers who
bury the bodies and hide them away, to prevent light
being thrown on the affair and to maintain this air of
mystery and mystification. Their complicity with the
powers-that-be is self-evident, for they are paid for the
work they do.

1ST CHARACTER. Many of them die too.

ORATOR. That's too bad for them. They are the lackeys
of the regime. Let us first seize the Council and its
officers.

2ND CHARACTER. Hurrah!

2ND & THIRD CHARACTERS. Bravo!

ORATOR. Follow me.

1ST, 2ND & 3RD CHARACTERS. Let's follow him! To the
Town Hall!

ORATOR. And if we meet any undertakers, we'll strike
them down.

(The ORATOR comes down from his platform, while the
THREE OTHER CHARACTERS SAY: 'Death to the
Councillors, death to the undertakers!')

Follow me!

(The ORATOR, with one arm raised, runs off to the
right. The THREE CHARACTERS run off after him
shouting: 'Kill them', and then reappear a second later)

1ST CHARACTER. He fell.

2ND CHARACTER. He fell stone dead.

3RD CHARACTER. They got him, the bastards!

1ST CHARACTER. He's a martyr to our just cause, a victim of objective chance.

2ND CHARACTER. They got him.

3RD CHARACTER. They got him. (They run away, crossing the stage and disappearing on the left)

STREET SCENE 2

(On the left-hand side of the stage another POLITICIAN is standing on a platform haranguing the crowd, that is to say the Audience, with THREE CHARACTERS in front of him)

ORATOR. Dear fellow citizens, ladies and gentlemen, in the agony that torments us we must think of the future. And not only of the future but also of the present. We must think of the survivors. Those who will survive are not inevitably other people. We ourselves may be the survivors. Each one of us is a possible survivor. Ladies, young ladies and gentlemen, I have called you together and you have come in defiance of the Council's orders. That some of us may be dying is no reason for us to sit and twiddle our thumbs. Even if the majority were to die, there would still be enough of us left to build up a world, a new world. The kingdom of heaven must be created on earth here in this very place, and we can construct, if not a great and perfect paradise, at least a little paradise with the smallest possible number of imperfections. I promise you social justice, in freedom. We have no wish to overthrow our present institutions, for we know what disasters can be brought by revolution. But we shall change everything. Or if not everything, at least a major part of things. We shall reduce the burden of taxation. The more of us die in this town, the more taxes we pay. We pay instead of the dead. That is not fair. Where does this money go? To the town's civil servants, the most numerous of whom are the undertakers, who have the highest salaries. If there are any undertakers among you here, you will still get paid if you vote for me. Not only shall we pay far lower taxes but we shall increase the wages of the workers and we shall lighten the burdens that weigh on our small traders. Our heads of commerce can no longer keep their businesses in good running order, because of excessive taxation. They too, in the same way as the workers, and the small, large and medium-sized traders, as well as the undertakers, will have a part of their load removed. As soon as the epidemic has ceased, we must all run to the ballot boxes, for we wish to act in full legality.

1ST CHARACTER. And the pensioners?

ORATOR. They will be looked after.

2ND CHARACTER. And the teachers?

ORATOR. They will be looked after.

3RD CHARACTER. And the farmers?

ORATOR. In view of the fact that there is little land to be cultivated within the walls of our city, we can quite easily, without depriving the other social groups, meet the needs of a reduced agricultural population, which the disease that afflicts us is alas still further reducing, and from one point of view this is a stroke of luck for those among the farmers who are going to survive.

Besides, my dear fellow citizens, the survivors in every social group will stand to gain considerably from the thinning out of the population. Not of course that I suggest that this is desirable. But if it must be accepted by necessity, we shall draw full advantage from it to the benefit of all. For I promise you happiness in a prosperous society of ever-increasing consumption, the advantages of poverty without its disadvantages. Happiness within the reach of all.

1ST CHARACTER. Bravo!

2ND CHARACTER. But how do you reconcile the

contradictions?

ORATOR. What contradictions?

2ND CHARACTER. (clearly retracting) Certain
   contradictions... How do you satisfy the workers and
   the bosses and trade interests all at the same time?

3RD CHARACTER (to the 2ND) Everyone just has to do his
   bit.

ORATOR. I have my plans. A twelve-point plan.

1ST CHARACTER. (to the 2ND) Reactionary! Fascist!

ORATOR. Are you then unable to recognise the psychological
   atmosphere that surrounds you? Think of the administrators
   we have! They are concerned only with death, with how to
   bury people, how to burn their effects in order to prevent
   the propagation of what perhaps is an epidemic and
   perhaps isn't one after all. Our rulers are obsessed with
   death, obsessed neurotics. They all add up to a regime
   that is morbid and decadent.

3RD CHARACTER. Down with a morbid and decadent regime!

1ST CHARACTER. Down with death-wishers! (To the 2ND
   CHARACTER) You're very quiet, don't you agree?

2ND CHARACTER. Why yes, I agree. Down with death-
   wishers!

ORATOR. According to our statistics three councillors are
   dead already. Two others are sick. How can we have
   confidence in rulers who set such a bad example to those
   they administer? I promise you governors who are as
   healthy as humanly possible and, within the limits of the
   human condition, immortal. I promise you happiness.

(Enter TWO POLICEMEN from the Right)

1ST POLICEMAN. Public assembly is forbidden.

2ND POLICEMAN. Disperse! Move along there!

ORATOR. Let all my flock disperse, let us disperse in orderly fashion, we shall conquer, but we shall conquer in full legality. (The ORATOR comes down from his platform. To the POLICEMEN) We are withdrawing against our will. I'll have my own back when we're in power. You will learn that we do not want a government which passes laws about death without a thought for the laws to pass about life. (The ORATOR, dignified, moves away, followed by the THREE CHARACTERS. To the THREE CHARACTERS) Follow me!

(The ORATOR and the THREE CHARACTERS back out slowly on the Left, singing)

ORATOR & 3 CHARACTERS. 'The time will come for our careers, the day that this lot are removed' (The tune is the 'Marseillaise'. They go out)

1ST POLICEMAN. Move along there!

2ND POLICEMAN. (pointing into the audience) Two dead men! (He staggers. The other POLICEMAN holds him up)

1ST POLICEMAN. He's ill. He has the signs. Ambulance!

(He goes off on the Left supporting the 2ND POLICEMAN. His shouts can be heard from the winds, mingling with the song sung by the other CHARACTERS)

THE COUNCIL CHAMBER

(A large table in the centre of the stage. A meeting of the Medical Officers of the town. There are THREE MEN and THREE WOMEN)

1ST DOCTOR. Our science is powerless.

2ND DOCTOR. Powerless with these cases. Powerless today. It will not be powerless tomorrow.

3RD DOCTOR. To say that science is powerless leads to

mysticism. And that is condemned by law. Or else to agnosticism, which is damned by the Medical Council, by the chemists, the physicists and the biologists, not to speak of the administration and committees of hygiene.

4TH DOCTOR. It is not mysticism that has littered the streets with corpses, with tens of thousands of corpses.

5TH DOCTOR. It is not science either, you know. They are dead because they failed to follow the precepts of hygiene.

2ND DOCTOR. Medical instruction in the universities as well as the teaching of hygiene and popular pre-medical treatment is wrongly conceived. In certain districts it is non-existent. The city's administration must be held responsible. The members of the municipal council should be arrested, the mayor and his officers as well as the other functionaries.

3RD DOCTOR. They must be judged and condemned to death.

1ST DOCTOR. For many of them, that's hardly worth the trouble.

4TH DOCTOR. Are you by any chance a supporter of mysticism? Yes, one does die through ignorance.

2ND DOCTOR. If one followed the precepts of medicine conscientiously from A to Z, no-one would die.

3RD DOCTOR. Theoretically only those people die who relax their vigilance and die unknowingly, without noticing, or else those who die are those who want to die, or those condemned to death, or soldiers killed in war.

4TH DOCTOR. People die in peacetime too. People die in spite of themselves. That's why many people, the polite ones, die apologising.

5TH DOCTOR. People die when they're willing to die. But this 'willing' to die is a complex sort of willing.

6TH DOCTOR. One dies when, consciously or not, one

accepts death. When the human being gives in and gives up. The valiant and those who struggle for freedom and self-determination should never give in.

1ST DOCTOR. You can't not give in.

2ND DOCTOR. You can and you must not give in.

3RD DOCTOR. If one dies, it's because one is willing to yield to the forces of evil. Death is reaction. It should not interfere with the forces of progress.

4TH DOCTOR. Yet we are all limited in time. That is a self-evident, that is an elementary truth. I deplore that death exists, but I equally deplore that you should have to be told so and that you are trying to deny this truth.

5TH DOCTOR. You deserve to be condemned to death. For as you resign yourself to death, we might just as well grant it you. A small tribunal, a swift judgment and that's it.

6TH DOCTOR. The surging masses do not fear death, it does not exist for those who have their heads screwed on, who have digested their doctrine and marched forward, always forward. Death is the temptation of reactionaries.

1ST DOCTOR. I share the view of my eminent colleague, the 4th Doctor here. At life's end waits inevitable death. Necessarily.

2ND DOCTOR. Our colleague should inform us what he means by 'necessarily'. There's no necessity about it. Except, of course, when men of law judge that certain citizens are guilty of crimes against humanity and their country. Or when medical authorities judge it no longer possible to provide for everybody's needs, and advise that twenty, thirty or forty per cent of the citizens should be liquidated. In such a case one executes all those and only those who believe in death for reasons of mysticism, all those who fail to obey the common laws of hygiene, or who set more store by death than they do by life. We have no need of them. It's just too bad!

75

4TH DOCTOR. We're all going to die, all living on borrowed time.

5TH DOCTOR. Prove it.

6TH DOCTOR. He'll never be able to produce the proof.

1ST DOCTOR. Come now, it's demonstrated by the laws of biology itself, not counting the enormous numbers of corpses, of people who were once sound in wind and limb and spirit.

2ND DOCTOR. All those who died died accidentally, of sickness or old age: the heart stops and the brain stops functioning. Theory and practice must have taught you that, something even a child is conscious of. One does not die when one is imbued with science, when one carries in one's head the theory and practice of our credo.

3RD DOCTOR. It was time that was restated.

4TH DOCTOR. So you maintain, ladies and gentlemen, that hundreds of thousands of people have died through ignorance, out of spite, or because they were unable to believe in the truth of our credo.

5TH DOCTOR. We can confirm that. They listened to counter-propaganda and became its victims. It's because of this counter-propaganda that our science lacks power. They are victims, but it is also their own fault. They should have believed us. Unfortunately they have a different belief, old and out of date, but still virulent.

6TH DOCTOR. Some people say that all action is useless, all revolution and all evolution too, for they say, whatever we do, death is waiting at the end.

1ST DOCTOR. That's an argument we should consider.

2ND DOCTOR. Could you be defeatists?

3RD DOCTOR. Could you be reactionaries?

4TH DOCTOR. I believe there is such a thing as death.

5TH DOCTOR. Shame on you.

6TH DOCTOR. I shall never die.

1ST DOCTOR. I bet you will.

2ND DOCTOR. (to the 1ST) The people who die are bad citizens.

3RD DOCTOR. The dying have been insufficiently politicised. We shall have to chastise their descendants.

4TH DOCTOR. Death is the only true alienation.

5TH DOCTOR. You're just formulating clichés.

6TH DOCTOR. (to the 1ST) Common sense brings us nothing but false truths. Between common sense and the truth there lies a gulf.

1ST DOCTOR. You don't wish to consider death. But death will consider us. We can't prevent it.

2ND DOCTOR. Untrue.

3RD DOCTOR. Untrue.

4TH DOCTOR. I should like to admit you are right. The heart is willing but my heart fails me. (He stands up) Excuse me. (He falls)

5TH DOCTOR. He's dead.

6TH DOCTOR. I'm not surprised.

1ST DOCTOR. I'm not surprised either.

2ND DOCTOR. But not for the same reasons.

3RD DOCTOR. It's his own fault. It's because he willed it. He sets a very bad example. Death is not the rule, it's the exception.

77

5TH DOCTOR. Bad examples are infectious.

6TH DOCTOR. The living are a mob foolish enough to follow bad examples. We'll know how to enlighten them.

1ST DOCTOR. It's the disease that's infectious. Excuse me.

(From the time of the 1ST DOCTOR's line: 'That's an argument we should consider', the text may be sung. Like a pseudo-opera)

I'm sorry. (He falls and dies)

2ND DOCTOR. You see.

3RD DOCTOR. You see.

5TH DOCTOR. You see.

6TH DOCTOR. You see.

2ND DOCTOR. He's only got what he deserves.

3RD DOCTOR. It's his belief in death that killed him. (End of the sung text)

5TH DICTOR. We shall prove that death does not exist for us.

6TH DOCTOR. We who believe in science and progress, we'll set a good example.

2ND DOCTOR. Down with death!

3RD DOCTOR. Long live life!

(The FOUR DOCTORS go out. Their voices can be heard from the wings. Pseudo-opera again)

5TH DOCTOR. Don't fall! (Noise of a fall)

6TH DOCTOR. Don't fall! (Noise of a fall)

2ND DOCTOR. Don't fall! (Noise of a fall)

3RD DOCTOR. That's enough now. Come now, don't fall!
I shall not fall. (Noise of a fall)

POLICEMAN'S VOICE. Ambulance! Ambulance!

(The voice of the POLICEMAN calling the ambulance
can still be heard when from the Right an OLD MAN
and an OLD WOMAN appear. The OLD MAN is
supporting the OLD WOMAN. They move slowly and with
some difficulty)

OLD WOMAN. It's such a beautiful day. Look at the sunset.
Isn't it beautiful? You don't say a word. Don't you like
the blue sky? Don't you like the sunset? You used to
in the old days.

OLD MAN. You always find everything beautiful: the
rain, the snow, the blue sky, the sun, the cobblestones
and the pavement.

OLD WOMAN. Everything is beautiful. Even the drains.

OLD MAN. Perhaps.

OLD WOMAN. Everything I see makes me happy.

OLD MAN. You are young, very young.

OLD WOMAN. Everything's a miracle. Every moment I
live brings enchantment.

OLD MAN. Once upon a time the world plunged me into
stupefaction. I too used to look about me - 'what is all
this?' - then I awoke from my stupor: 'Who was I?'.
And I was stupefied afresh to look inside myself. I was
too full of this world. Too full of this me: I couldn't not
say so - not shout it out. Who to? To myself, for
myself, and then it seemed for others. This question is
above all for oneself alone. One asks it of oneself.
Absolute solitude interrogating an unpeopled universe.
Finally, after 'What is all this', after 'What am I', 'Who

am I', came the 'Why am I here surrounded by all this'. This third one is already not so perfect a question. Not so metaphysical, more practical, more historical. But already in the earlier stupefaction there had been a feeling of menace, this world and myself troubled me and filled me with terror. It is with this our life begins. It's fascinating so long as the question-mark exists. Then one stops questioning, one gets tired. Only the menace remains, the gnawing anxiety. The world becomes familiar and quite natural. All that is left is weariness, boredom and that fear which is still there, which alone has been there since the beginning. Life is no longer a miracle, it's a nightmare. I don't know how you've been able to guard your miracle intact. For me each moment is both empty and too heavy. Everything is terrible. I sink into an anguish of boredom.

OLD WOMAN. How can one be bored? The trees, are they bored? The road is not bored. The lakes reflect the sky and unite with it.

OLD MAN. Furniture gets bored. The walls sweat boredom. The doors are sad. Open, they shout at you. Shut, they creak or groan.

OLD WOMAN. The plants open to the light. The leaves are never brittle. Every face I see I stroke with my eyes.

OLD MAN. Faces close in upon themselves. Besides, I repel all those eyes. Heads are like chopping-blocks. And all is dark and dingy. Think of the stones: there they are, in their prison, crushed beneath a weight of silence.

OLD WOMAN. Stones have faces too. They can smile and sing.

OLD MAN. Everything has withered. I have withered. I'm two hundred years old. I've waited all this time to come alive. Alas, I'll wait no longer. Nothing left to wait for, except nothing.

OLD WOMAN. Your sadness is the only withering my heart endures: it is my only wound. How can you not be happy when I am near you? Your presence is enough for me, surrounded by the universe. I tell myself that you exist and thank you.

OLD MAN. All that time... All the time we've been here!

OLD WOMAN. Nothing has changed since the very first day, and my love renews itself. Every day for me is the very first day. A first day that I welcome every day. I've been content with this mysterious presence of the world, with all that's around me and an awareness of existence. I have never felt the need to know more. Every question pierces the living soul and wounds it. Every question questions everything. To ask questions is to refuse, even if one does not know one is refusing. To ask questions is not to trust or to be empty inside. But it's a matter of temperament, of course. Since one's birth one has chosen whether it's to be refusal or acceptance. If you were content, there'd not be a cloud in my sky. I'd dance and shout for joy, if that's what you wanted, if you let me I'd sweep you off your feet with ecstasy. Let's dance.

(They go on advancing with difficulty)

Every morning is brand new. With every dawn the world is born again, all spotless and virgin bright. If you're so sad you cannot love me enough.

OLD MAN. I love nothing. But you, I love you. I love you in my fashion. I love you as best I may. As much as I can. With all the strength that's left me.

OLD WOMAN. You can't love me much, not much above indifference.

OLD MAN. Yes I do. Because after all I need you.

OLD WOMAN. All I need is you. With just a snatch of sky, a touch of light, a scrap of shade, and perhaps a little warmth.

OLD MAN. So you don't look around you then? What reasons can we find to be gay and happy?

OLD WOMAN. It's you who don't know how to look.

OLD MAN. It's you.

OLD WOMAN. You don't look far enough. No, we won't start bickering!

OLD MAN. How did you accept this anguish? Everyone around us is frightened. Trapped in their own misery.

OLD WOMAN. You've always been frightened. Even when there was no reason to be scared. Leave people to their fears. They must cure themselves of their fears.

OLD MAN. Yes. I have always been in anguish. It's not so much other people's fear that weighs on me, my own anguish is enough. Today I can see it reflected in the eyes of everyone. It gets multiplied.

OLD WOMAN. My leg hurts a little.

OLD MAN. Are you tired?

OLD WOMAN. It's nothing. Give me your arm.

OLD MAN. Once, a long time ago, I used to fight my grief. There were founts of joy within me which I thought inexhaustible, springs of life. Joy would fight my anguish. What energy I had! What youth! What wealth! Strong was the anguish for sure, but my vitality was stronger. Who would have thought I should grow so old so fast? As I grew older, you grew younger. For me a second lasts a year, a year is just a second.

OLD WOMAN. I learnt the lesson of love, my dear. I love you more and more, each day a little more. And you're the only one I cannot understand, that's why I have such sorrow loving you.

OLD MAN. How long is it going on? I have been in the world for centuries, yet it's merely a moment. Such a long time, so short a while. The load gets harder to bear. Everything is dark.

82

OLD WOMAN. It could get lighter all the time. I could get lighter still, there'd be no weight at all if it weren't for your distress. That is my only load. Take things easier. Oh! look at that shop and the lovely dresses!

OLD MAN. We can't accept our condition. I can no longer live in this city. Locked in. I can no longer live in our house. Locked in. I've a horror of home. Of every home. You get locked in. Locked up. I don't want to go home and yet I know I shall.

OLD WOMAN. If only you'd known what you were looking for! You've never known. My love. The pain you cause me. I love you.

(The words of love she speaks and the revolt that he expresses are uttered in the voices of old people, of course, rather cracked)

OLD MAN. Yes, yes, we love each other, we do. But I'm afraid I can't live outside either. If I go out, it's only to come home. If I come home, it's only to go out. Every time time I left home, it was only to come back. Returning, coming back to oneself. I come back and always find myself. It has always been like that. But at least there was a coming and going. Now, alas, my legs give way, my arms drop to my sides. I fall... You're not going to fall!

OLD WOMAN. (nearly falling as the OLD MAN prevents her) A little faint. Forgive me. I don't know what's wrong. It will pass.

OLD MAN. Don't you feel well? Do you want a rest?

OLD WOMAN. I think it's over. Let's go on with our walk. I so like walking arm in arm with you.

OLD MAN. Going for a walk is a bore. But the house is unbearable. I'm too restless to stay still, whether I'm sitting, lying or standing. I want to run about. So tiring.

OLD WOMAN. The world is deep and sweet. It's nice to be

in the street, in the avenues. It's nice to stand by the window at home.

OLD MAN. The universe is a great steel globe, impenetrable. It was once a meadow covered in flowers, poisoned flowers, but flowers all the same. I used to run through the grass, through the corn, to the river's edge, chasing my dreams.

OLD WOMAN. Even then you were wild. Running does no good. You scarcely have to bend down to pick them. Everything is within our reach. It does no good to try and chase after dreams. They catch hold of us. We ourselves are as if in a dream.

OLD MAN. I've wasted my life.

OLD WOMAN. I'll win it back for you, if I win you. Why do you resist me so, my dear? Why don't you know how to take? Why don't you dare?

OLD MAN. I thought I was born to be victorious and free. I didn't dare. I never dared go on to the end. I could never make up my mind.

OLD WOMAN. You never really wished to with all your heart.

OLD MAN. I only went on to the end of the labour. To the end of the ages. Why did I never conquer the moment? Why did I never conquer the stars? Why is the universe so sullen with me?

OLD WOMAN. I still hope you'll learn about love. I still hope so for your sake.

OLD MAN. (ironically) Of course, so long as we're not snuffed out. (Short pause) To be completely free, to live. Now I'm no longer interested. That's what might have cured me.

OLD WOMAN. I'll help you. So long as my strength lasts.

OLD MAN. I'm no longer interested. I want nothing now.

Only not to have to endure this boring grief which devours me.

OLD WOMAN. You're ill, my dear. But I still hope for you. Still hope. (Suddenly she feels ill) I've a sore throat. I've a sore head.

OLD MAN. You're staggering.

OLD WOMAN. It's nothing. Never fear.

OLD MAN. (supporting her) You're getting weak, my darling, you can hardly stand up!

OLD WOMAN. Stomach ache. Like a burning fire.

OLD MAN. Lean on me. Let's go home.

OLD WOMAN. Don't be frightened.

OLD MAN. Fight back, I beg you, I'll carry you. Come along, I'll look after you.

OLD WOMAN. I'm stifling. Hold me tight. But it will pass, I've had this before.

OLD MAN. Never, she's never been so bad. You've never been so ill. Help us, God! She has the marks of the scourge, she has the signs.

OLD WOMAN. Help me. Don't get upset. Let's go quietly home. I'll have a lie down and you can stay close to me. It will pass. You'll be cured too.

(She is about to fall. He supports her with difficulty)

OLD MAN. (dragging himself forward with the OLD WOMAN) My darling. You promised to stay with me till the end of our days. You can't leave me, you promised. You mustn't. You can't. Who is there to help us, except God! And he's not there.

OLD WOMAN. Take me away and I'll take you away.

OLD MAN. The house isn't far.

OLD WOMAN. It's so far. But I'll manage. As you're there.

OLD MAN. A little courage, my darling, my little love.
You must have enough for the two of us, as I have none
left.

OLD WOMAN. Yes, that's it, I'll lie down. And you can lie
down next to me. We'll be side by side. That's happiness.
We'll be cured. We still have a long, long time to spend
together...to live.

OLD MAN. Don't leave me. Don't leave me. You mustn't.
I have you and I'll keep you. How was it I didn't understand?

OLD WOMAN. We understand each other...

OLD MAN. It's too late. We're going to be swallowed in
the night. Joy was here, and I never knew. Come, little
girl, let me take you away. And you can carry me with
you into your night.

OLD WOMAN. There'll be a few moments.

(He goes off with her to the Left, almost dragging her)

OLD MAN. Help me, friends, brothers!

(They have gone out)

(Street scene)

THE PUBLIC OFFICIAL. (followed by the THREE WOMEN
who surround him and almost cling to him) I tell you I
can do nothing for you.

1ST WOMAN. There's no more flour, not one lump of
sugar left.

2ND WOMAN. And not a single drop of oil.

86

OFFICIAL. I can't help you. Economise. You know very well we can't get more supplies. We're besieged, blockaded. Where do you expect me to find oil for you? I can't become bread. I can't just become sugar. (He tries to free himself)

3RD WOMAN. (holding a baby in her arms) In our district, the poor areas, starvation kills as many as disease.

1ST WOMAN. More die of starvation.

OFFICIAL. You've got used to it then.

2ND WOMAN. There are still provisions in the wealthy districts.

3RD WOMAN. The posh areas have supplies. They don't lack anything.

OFFICIAL. Because they know how to economise. They didn't rush and devour the food like the voracious creatures you are. They saved some up. That's why they've still got some.

1ST WOMAN. They had the means to stock up with. They could pile up their stores as much as they liked.

OFFICIAL. You are privileged. It's better to die of hunger than of plague.

2ND WOMAN. The reserves should be shared out equally. I'd rather die of disease.

3RD WOMAN. Fair shares.

1ST, 2ND & 3RD WOMEN. Fair shares! Fair shares!

OFFICIAL. That's against the law. Each district has its depot. The administration does not authorise the transport of stores from one district to another.

1ST WOMAN. We want bread.

2ND WOMAN. (indicating the OFFICIAL) Let's eat <u>him</u>.

OFFICIAL. Help! (He struggles and breaks away) Help!

(He has escaped on Audience Right. Centre Stage the
1ST and 2ND WOMEN fall on the 3RD WOMAN and try
to snatch her baby)

1ST WOMAN. Let's share the baby. A little child's flesh
is far better than that official's! A hide like a mule!

3RD WOMAN. Help! My baby!

(The 1ST and 2ND WOMEN run off with the baby in their
arms, fighting each other for it)

1ST WOMAN. It's mine.

2ND WOMAN. It was my idea.

3RD WOMAN. My baby! Give me back my child! (She
rushes at the other TWO WOMEN shouting) My baby!
(In the scrimmage, the child passes from one to the
other)

1ST WOMAN. It's for me.

2ND WOMAN. It's for me.

(They leave the stage struggling over the baby and almost
at once the 3RD WOMAN reappears, running half-way
across the stage. Then she stops, holding in her arms the
child she has succeeded in wresting from the other TWO
WOMEN)

3RD WOMAN. My pet, my little darling, I saved you. (She
makes for the exit, Audience Right, kissing her baby)
They hurt you, sweetheart, didn't they, they hurt you.

(Behind her, coming from the back of the stage, a MAN
strides silently after her. The blade of a knife flashes
in his hand and he drives it into the back of the 3RD
WOMAN. She falls screaming, still holding her child and
clutching it to her. The MAN takes the child from the
arms of the murdered WOMAN and runs off with it.
ANOTHER MAN arrives with ANOTHER MAN or WOMAN.

They run to the body of the 3RD WOMAN and carry it
off towards the wings, Audience Left)

MAN. A dead woman. Quite fresh.

2ND MAN OR WOMAN. She's very skinny.

(They lift the dead WOMAN up)

Still she's more tender than a man.

(They disappear, while ANOTHER WOMAN enters
Audience Right and slowly crosses the stage to the Left.
She is holding a tray full of rissoles)

WOMAN. Little meat rissoles, piping hot! Come and get
them! Little rissoles, nice and fresh. Minced meat
rissoles, tender and true! Come and buy my rissoles,
a dozen for one hundred francs, thirteen to the dozen.
(She goes off on the Left, still crying:) More tender
than lamb, flesh as fresh as a daisy. Come and taste
my rissoles.

(She has gone out, but can still be heard crying 'Come
and taste!' At the same time TWO CHARACTERS, MEN
or WOMEN, or a MAN and a WOMAN, come in from the
Right)

1ST CHARACTER. Anthropophagi?

2ND CHARACTER. Why yes, anthropophagi.

1ST CHARACTER. But of course not, not professionals,
they're not professionals. Amateurs? Not even that. It's
just on occasion. One's not anthropophagous just because
two or three husbands have eaten their wives, or because
a few odd parents, under pressure, eat a child. Still, I
advise you to watch out that none of the humans, great or
small, that get eaten up have caught the disease. As a
simple preventive measure. A case of salubrity, shall
we say? If one eats someone who has the sickness, one
falls sick oneself. It's running a great risk. But if, when
lashed by hunger...you take a fancy...to some <u>bon
viveur</u>...well, throughout history it has been known when

89

times are hard.

2ND CHARACTER. Why yes, indeed, it can't be helped, can it, if then we eat each other.

1ST CHARACTER. It's only human, after all, it's only human. It's on account of the sickness we've been reduced to this. Objective necessity. Otherwise, normally, we love or hate each other without eating each other. But I myself, in spite of everything, I'm chary of food. I'm chary, because of the disease.

2ND CHARACTER. The disease is in everything, you know. Anyway, you live in a wealthy zone, you've still got all you need.

(They go out Audience Left. TWO CHARACTERS enter from the Right)

1ST CHARACTER. If you want boots, follow me.

(The 2ND CHARACTER hesitates)

Why do you hesitate? Do you really want them?

2ND CHARACTER. (hesitating) Yes, yes, of course.

1ST CHARACTER. What are you afraid of? There's no sickness at my place. The boots are at home, where else do you think I keep them? (He approaches a door at the rear of the stage) Well? Do you want to come up or not? (He gives him a slight push) Let you have the boots for two chunks of bread. Look! You'll have boots like mine. (The 1ST CHARACTER has indeed got beautiful boots on) Two kilos of bread.

2ND CHARACTER. But these boots... are they...?

1ST CHARACTER. Yes, don't worry, they're disinfected. (He knocks at the door, which is opened) I've brought you one, all alive-o! Looks healthy too!

(A MAN comes out, knife in hand. With his other hand he pulls the 2ND CHARACTER towards him, while the

1ST CHARACTER pushes him inside. The door is quickly closed as one hears a scream from the 2ND CHARACTER.

From the Left comes a cart, drawn perhaps by the BLACK MONK. It is full of bodies. A WOMAN or A MAN rushes to the cart which continues on to the Right. Then ANOTHER MAN tries to pull one of the bodies off the cart. They have almost pulled it off as they disappear on the Right. From the Right enters a MAN brandishing two heads. He runs off Left pursued by a POLICEMAN blowing his whistle)

(For a few moments, in a corner of the stage, on the right, a group of FOUR WOMEN have been spying on them. A burial cart appears from the left. It is drawn by TWO ACTORS as horses with a MUTE on either side. The cart is preceded by the MONK IN BLACK, who crosses the stage and goes off on the right in silence. The cart moves towards the shop at the rear of the stage)

1ST MUTE. Gee up!

2ND MUTE. Gee up! Go on, you donkey!

1ST WOMAN. It's in the shop.

1ST MUTE. Where are the bodies?

2ND WOMAN. They're in the dress shop.

3RD WOMAN. They're lying on the counter.

4TH WOMAN. They were too rich.

1ST WOMAN. They've eaten enough and drunk enough.

2ND WOMAN. Eaten too much and drunk too much.

1ST MUTE. (opening the door of the shop) Not a pretty sight!

(He enters)

2ND MUTE. I'll look after the woman. You take the man.

3RD WOMAN. They weren't very nice people.

4TH WOMAN. Don't waste pity on them.

1ST WOMAN. They didn't think of the poor.

2ND WOMAN. I won't pay them my debts now.

(The FOUR WOMEN have approached the entrance to the shop)

3RD WOMAN. They were cousins of my husband's. Good riddance. My husband is dead too.

4TH WOMAN. Good riddance.

(The TWO MUTES come out. One with the WOMAN slung over his shoulder, the other with the MAN. They throw the bodies into the cart. The WOMEN fall back)

1ST MUTE. They must have conked out two days ago.

2ND MUTE. (to the WOMEN) Go on, make way!

1ST MUTE. Move along! Or I'll chuck them at you!

(The FOUR WOMEN rush off to the four corners of the stage)

1ST WOMAN. (to the MUTES) I was the one who informed you.

2ND MUTE. No reward for that! Move out of the way and then stay where you are!

1ST MUTE. (to the 2ND) Ouf! They were fat and greasy.

2ND MUTE. (to the 1ST) Soup-sellers full of soup!

1ST MUTE. Flower-sellers, hat-sellers.

2ND MUTE. (to the horse) Gee up!

1ST MUTE. Use your whip.

(Accompanying the cart they go out on the Right)

1ST WOMAN. They've gone.

2ND WOMAN. Looting is forbidden.

3RD WOMAN. That won't worry us.

(The THREE WOMEN enter the shop)

4TH WOMAN. It won't worry me either.

(The 4TH WOMAN goes into the shop. The MONK
enters again and crosses the stage in the opposite direction
from last time. He goes out. The 1ST WOMAN comes out
of the shop with an enormous flowery hat)

1ST WOMAN. When I think how long I've coveted this.

(The 2ND WOMAN comes out of the shop with dresses over
her arms)

2ND WOMAN. Dresses! And a hat!

3RD WOMAN. (coming out of the shop) Jewellery and
artificial flowers and such a lovely necklace.

4TH WOMAN. (coming out of the shop) Hats, hats, hats
galore!

(They take off their old dresses and get themselves up
in the clothes and hats they have taken. They were
dressed in black before, now we see them putting on
dresses and hats of every colour. They have armfuls
of things. Some fall to the ground and they quarrel over
them. They shout at each other. They have sunshades and
umbrellas too)

THE FOUR WOMEN. That's mine! No, it's mine! You've
never looked so well dressed! I'm not out of the gutter!
That's mine! Won't he be surprised when he sees me!
He will be pleased! That necklace is mine! I love flowery

hats! I love green dresses! That doesn't suit you! Green suits me to perfection! Pity there's no mirror! My feathers! To hell with your feathers!

(They look sumptuously grotesque and the feathers fly all over the stage. They quarrel over things. They all have hats in different colours. The stage is strewn with an incredible quantity of finery)

1ST WOMAN. Serve them right!

2ND WOMAN. They're not so mean now!

3RD WOMAN. This'll save us some money!

4TH WOMAN. Now we're dressed like rich folk.

(Enter a 5TH WOMAN from the Left)

5TH WOMAN. (to all the others) Thieves!

1ST WOMAN. Why don't you take some, what's it matter to you?

5TH WOMAN. They were my aunt and uncle, I'm their legal heiress.

2ND WOMAN. It's public property now.

5TH WOMAN. Give me my hats and dresses back.

3RD WOMAN. Come and get them!

5TH WOMAN. I'll go and complain to the police.

4TH WOMAN. We had official permission.

5TH WOMAN. Liar!

(She rushes from one to the other of the FOUR WOMEN and picks up some of the things that have fallen. She gets beaten with the sunshades. She dresses herself up too with whatever she can lay her hands on. It's a confusion of shouts and squeals and scuffles. Countless

flowers and feathers fly in all directions. All this
should make a very colourful tableau vivant as they are
all dressed in the stolen articles. The 2ND, then the
3RD WOMAN go into the shop and come out bringing
more dresses and hats and throwing other objects all
over the place. This all happens at a very fast pace)

FINAL SCENE.

From Audience left a public OFFICIAL comes on, followed
by the rest of the company who arrive individually from
both sides and gradually fill up the stage. The new arrivals
mingle with the ladies in their hats)

OFFICIAL. (who comes running on) Dear fellow citizens,
ladies and gentlemen, listen to me, citizens, ladies,
comrades, brothers, sisters, listen to me! I have
great news to announce to you. Listen to me, listen!

A MAN. Listen to him!

A WOMAN. What new disaster is he going to announce?

ANOTHER WOMAN. For weeks and weeks, for months and
months, the authorities have done nothing but promise
misfortune.

3RD MAN. Down with the authorities!

3RD WOMAN. Down with the authorities!

4TH WOMAN. (singing) Down with the authorities!

ALL THE WOMEN AND
TWO MEN IN CHORUS. Down with the authorities!

OFFICIAL. Listen to me!

4TH MAN. Listen to him!

5TH WOMAN. It's the fault of the authorities!

6TH WOMAN. They're the assassins!

OFFICIAL. Listen to me! Listen to me!

5TH MAN. No-one's responsible for our pitiful state.

CHORUS OF MEN. (sung) It's not the responsibility of anyone.

OFFICIAL. Listen!

6TH MAN. Our sins and our vices are the cause of our distress.

CHORUS OF MEN. (sung) It's we who are responsible.

CHORUS OF WOMEN. (sung) We are not responsible.

OFFICIAL. Listen to me!

6TH, 7TH & 8TH WOMEN. (pointing their fingers at the 6TH, 7TH & 8TH MEN) It's your fault, it's your fault!

6TH, 7TH & 8TH WOMEN. (pointing their fingers at the WOMEN, singing) It's your fault, it's your fault!

OFFICIAL. Listen to me! Listen!

5TH WOMAN. (to the OFFICIAL) We won't listen to you any more.

(End of sung text)

1ST MAN. No-one's guilty.

2ND MAN. It's not that we've been punished. We are the victims of an absurd disease. It has no moral significance.

OFFICIAL. Listen to me! (Sung:) Listen, can't you!

1ST WOMAN. It's the council's fault.

6TH MAN. It's the fault of those fat, pot-bellied bourgeois. They lived lives of luxurious lust, now we have to pay for their gluttony.

6TH WOMAN. Their vices.

1ST WOMAN. And their sins.

7TH WOMAN. Their lack of charity.

8TH MAN. Their lust.

6TH MAN. Their atheism.

6TH WOMAN. It's not the fault of the rich, it's the fault of the poor.

7TH WOMAN. They're dirty.

8TH WOMAN. Because they're unhygienic.

1ST WOMAN. Because of those poor and dirty old drunkards.

OFFICIAL. Listen to me! Listen! (Sung)

CHORUS OF MEN, EXCEPT
FOR 1ST & 2ND MEN. (sung) It's the fault of the rich.

CHORUS OF WOMEN. (sung) It's the fault of the poor.

OFFICIAL. Listen to me!

1ST MAN. Why won't you listen to him!

OFFICIAL. I have some good news to announce.

5TH, 6TH, 7TH & 8TH MEN
& THE CHORUS OF WOMEN. It's the fault of the authorities!
Down with the authorities!

2ND MAN. He's going to announce some good news!

THE OTHER MEN. He's going to announce some good news!

1ST WOMAN. He says he's going to announce some good news!

3RD WOMAN. It seems it's good news!

OFFICIAL. Listen!

CHORUS OF MEN. Listen!

CHORUS OF WOMEN. Listen!

OFFICIAL. Dear citizens, ladies and gentlemen. Our statistics tell us that the disease is on the decline, declining very fast. At a gallop! In the 23rd District last week there were 50,000 dead. This week no more than three.

4TH WOMAN. It seems the disease is on the wane.

3RD MAN. The disease is on the wane.

OFFICIAL. In the 15th District last week there were 90,000 dead. Now there are no more than three. In the 1st Distric last week there were 80,000 dead, and this week no-one has died. And in our own District one victim of the plague has been cured. There were no dead at all.

1ST WOMAN. No-one's dying now.

1ST MAN. Except the disease.

2ND MAN. We want a full assurance of that.

3RD WOMAN. Assurance.

4TH WOMAN. Assurance.

5TH WOMAN. Assurance.

OFFICIAL. The administration has never kept you from reality. In our darkest hour, we showed you the statistics. We'll never hide from you the number of dead and dying. We've done all we could to wipe out the disease by taking severe and even unpopular measures. We have no reason to lie today.

5TH WOMAN. Proof!

6TH MAN. We demand proof!

OFFICIAL. You have proof. Since I arrived no-one has died. No-one will die any more. I give you my word of honour.

1ST MAN. He gives us his word of honour.

2ND MAN. Long live the authorities! Long live the administration!

1ST WOMAN. We are so relieved.

5TH MAN. We are saved.

3RD MAN. Bravo!

THE MEN AND WOMEN. Hurrah!

(They go out shouting hurrah and kissing one another. An outburst of joy. This scene of mad gaiety should last about one minute. The OFFICIAL is borne aloft in triumph. Then, suddenly, at the rear of the stage can be seen the glow of a fire which will spread over the whole stage and set it ablaze)

A WOMAN. Fire!

A MAN. There's a fire!

(The OFFICIAL is unceremoniously dropped, but rises hastily to his feet again)

A MAN. There's a fire!

A WOMAN. To the fire!

ANOTHER MAN. To the fire! Help!

A MAN. Help!

A WOMAN. Run for it!

A MAN. The fire's coming from the rich districts!

A WOMAN. It's not true, it's coming from the poor districts!

OFFICIAL. Let's escape that way! (He points to the right)

A WOMAN. We can't!

A MAN. We can't go that way, it's a sea of flames!

OFFICIAL. Let's go this way!

> (They all make off towards the left. Cries of 'The fire's there too!')

> (Indicating the rear of the stage) That way!

THE MEN. (running to the rear of the stage and shouting) This way!

A MAN. Not there either!

ANOTHER MAN. We're caught in a trap. Like rats.

> (They all turn and make for the front of the stage, then turn round again shouting: 'Fire, fire, we're all going to burn, fire, fire!' The BLACK MONK enters from Audience right. Of all the people who come in contact with him, no-one sees him. He goes and stands in the middle of the stage)

> (In front of the curtain appears a character of middle age, of middle size, and to judge by his clothes, of middle class. He addresses the Audience)

MAN. (in a loud voice) Ladies and gentlemen. Young ladies. (Then, suddenly he stops, his hands to his stomach, and writhes in pain) Oooooooh! Excuse me.

> (He is about to collapse when the curtain opens and TWO TOUGH MEN take him in their arms. Through the open curtain you can see a table on which there is a coffin in which they put the dead man. The TWO TOUGH MEN close the coffin and carry it off, leaving the stage as the Audience starts applauding)

THE OVERSIGHT

THE OVERSIGHT was first performed as LA LACUNE on March 7th, 1966, at L'Odéon-Théâtre de France, with the following cast:

THE FRIEND	Jean Dessailly
THE ACADEMICIAN	Pierre Bertin
HIS WIFE	Madeleine Renaud

The play was directed by Jean-Louis Barrault.

(Scene: an upper-class drawing room that is also somewhat 'artistic'. At least one sofa and several armchairs, one of which is green, French Regency style, right in the centre of the room. The walls are covered with enormous framed diplomas on which can be read in large letters the words: 'Doctor Honoris Causa'. The rest of the print is less clearly visible. On other diplomas can be seen the words: 'Doctorate Honoris Causa', and on other smaller ones: 'Doctorate', 'Doctorate', 'Doctorate', 'Doctorate'. One door on Audience Right. When the curtain rises, the Academician's WIFE is on stage. Wearing a simple negligee-type dressing-gown, she has doubtless just left her bed without having had the time to dress. Opposite her is the FRIEND, smartly clad, holding his hat and umbrella, in stiff white collar, dark jacket, striped trousers and black shoes)

WIFE. Well, my dear friend, tell me quickly!

FRIEND. I hardly know how to break it to you.

WIFE. I've guessed!

FRIEND. I've known the news since yesterday evening. I didn't wish to telephone you. But I couldn't wait any longer. Forgive me for dragging you out of bed to announce a thing like this.

WIFE. He couldn't manage it! What a disaster! We were hoping till the very last moment.

FRIEND. I understand. It's very hard on you. Yet there was some chance for him. Not much, really. We should have expected it.

WIFE. I wasn't expecting it. He was successful in everything. He always pulled through at the last minute.

FRIEND. Exhausted as he was! You should never have let
him do it.

WIFE. What could I do? How could I know?... It's terrible.

FRIEND. Take heart, my dear! That's life!

WIFE. I don't feel very well. I'm afraid I'm going to faint.
(She drops into an armchair)

FRIEND. (helping her and tapping her hands and cheeks) The
way I told you, it was much too brutal. Forgive me.

WIFE. You were quite right, you had to. One way or other I
had to know.

FRIEND. Would you like a glass of water? (He calls:) A
glass of water! (To the WIFE) I should have had more
consideration for your feelings.

WIFE. That wouldn't have altered the facts. (The MAID
enters with a glass of water)

MAID. What's happened? Is Madam not feeling well?

FRIEND. (taking the glass) Leave us, I'll give it to her.
She'll be all right. I had to bring her bad news.

MAID. Oh, not...Monsieur?

FRIEND. (to the MAID) Yes. You knew?

MAID. I hadn't heard. But now, by the way you look, I
understand.

FRIEND. Leave us alone. (The MAID goes off, quite upset,
muttering: 'The poor Master!' To the WIFE) Do you feel
better?

WIFE. I must be strong. I'm thinking about him, poor man!
I hope they won't mention it in the papers. Can one count

104

on the discretion of journalists?

FRIEND. Don't open the door. And don't answer the
telephone.

WIFE. The news will still get around.

FRIEND. You can go off to the country. In a few months,
when you've quite recovered, you'll come back and pick
up your life again. People forget.

WIFE. They won't forget this so quickly. It's just what they've
been waiting for. A few of our friends will swallow it,
but the rest, the rest...

(Enter the ACADEMICIAN in uniform, sword at his side,
his chest covered in decorations down to the belt)

ACADEMICIAN. Oh, you're awake? (To the FRIEND) You're
an early caller. What's the matter? Have you heard the
result?

WIFE. It's shameful!

FRIEND. (to the WIFE) Don't reproach him, my dear! (To
the ACADEMICIAN) You've failed.

ACADEMICIAN. Are you sure?

FRIEND. You should never have tried for your
baccalaureate.

ACADEMICIAN. Failed my bac! The rotten swine! They
dared do that to me!

FRIEND. They put the results up very late in the evening.

ACADEMICIAN. If it was dark, perhaps no-one could read
them? How were you able to?

FRIEND. There were spotlights.

ACADEMICIAN. They do all they can to compromise me.

FRIEND. I went back this morning. The lists were still there.

ACADEMICIAN. You should have suborned the concierge to take them down.

FRIEND. That's just what I did. But I'm afraid the police were there. Your name headed the list of candidates who failed. There's a queue of people fighting to see.

ACADEMICIAN. Who? The pupils' parents?

FRIEND. Others as well.

WIFE. All your rivals must be there, your colleagues. All the ones you attacked in the press for their ignorance Your old pupils, your students, all those postgraduates turned down because of you, when you were President of the Board.

ACADEMICIAN. It's the dishonour! But they shan't get away with it. Maybe it's a mistake.

FRIEND. I've seen the examiners. Spoken to them. They gave me your marks. Nought in mathematics.

ACADEMICIAN. I'm not a scientist.

FRIEND. Nought in Greek. Nought in Latin.

WIFE. (to her husband) You, a humanist! The official spokesman for Humanism! Author of 'The Defence and Apologia of Humanism'!

ACADEMICIAN. (to the FRIEND) But the French, my mark for French Composition?

FRIEND. You were given nine hundred. Nine hundred marks.

ACADEMICIAN. But that's perfect. It makes up for the other subjects.

FRIEND. I'm afraid not! It's marked out of two thousand.

You need a thousand to pass.

ACADEMICIAN. They've changed the system!

WIFE. They didn't change it just on your account. You always think you're being persecuted.

ACADEMICIAN. They have, they've changed the system.

FRIEND. They've gone back to the old one, from Napoleon's time.

ACADEMICIAN. That's old-fashioned. Anyway, when did they alter it, that regulation? It's not legal. I'm the President of the National Ministry of Education's Commission for the Baccalaureate. They didn't consult me. And they can't change it without my accord. I'll attack them in the Council of State!

WIFE. You don't know what you're talking about, darling. You're gaga. You know you gave in your resignation, before taking the exam, so there could be no doubt of the examiners' objectivity.

ACADEMICIAN. I'll withdraw my resignation.

FRIEND. That's a childish thing to say. You know that's impossible.

WIFE. I'm not surprised you failed any more! It's hardly a mature thing to do, to take a teenage exam with the mentality of a child.

ACADEMICIAN. To think I went in for that exam with two hundred other candidates who could have been my children!

FRIEND. Don't exaggerate. You can't be the father of hundreds of students.

ACADEMICIAN. I don't find much comfort in that!

WIFE. You should never have taken it. I told you not to. I knew it wouldn't do. You must have every qualification that's going. Never satisfied. What did you need this one for? Now all is lost. It's pretty disastrous, anyway. You have your doctorate, you have your degree, your elementary certificate, your pass in primary studies, and you even have the first part of your bac!

ACADEMICIAN. There was a gap.

WIFE. Nobody knew.

ACADEMICIAN. I did. I knew. Others could have found out. When I went to the Faculty Office to ask for a duplicate copy of my degree diploma, I was told: 'Why yes, of course, Mr. President, Mr. Dean, Mr. Academician...' And then they started searching. The Registrar came back looking rather embarrassed, very embarrassed in fact, and he said: 'There's something funny, a very strange thing, you got your degree all right, but it's no longer valid.' Naturally I asked him why, and he replied: 'There's a gap before your degree. I don't know how it could have happened. You were accepted by the Faculty of Arts without having the second part of your baccalaureate.'

FRIEND. And so?

WIFE. Your degree is no longer valid?

ACADEMICIAN. No. At least, not completely. It's been suspended. 'You'll receive the duplicate you ask for if you take your baccalaureate. You'll pass of course.' So I was really obliged to take it.

WIFE. You weren't obliged to at all. Why did you go rummaging about in the archives? In your position, you had no need of this qualification. No-one asked you for anything.

ACADEMICIAN. In point of fact, when the Registrar told me I didn't have my bac, I told him it wasn't possible. I wasn't too sure myself. I made a great effort to remember. Did I take my baccalaureate? Or didn't I? And then, in the end, I remembered that indeed I didn't take it. Now I recall that I had a cold that day.

WIFE. You had one of your usual hangovers, you mean.

FRIEND. Your husband, my dear, wanted to fill a gap. He's conscientious.

WIFE. You don't know him! It's not that at all. It's glory he's after, with honours. He never has enough. He wanted to hang that diploma on the walls, his degree diploma, with dozens of others. What does one diploma matter, more or less? No-one notices them. Only he comes and contemplates them, at night. I've often caught him at it. He gets up, tiptoes into this drawing-room, gazes at them and counts them up.

ACADEMICIAN. What else can I do when I can't sleep?

FRIEND. The questions for the bac are usually known in advance. You were admirably well placed to find them out. You could equally well have delegated someone to sit the exam in your place. One of your pupils. Or if you wanted to sit yourself, without it being known that you'd seen the questions in advance, you could have sent the maid to buy them on the black market, where they're always available.

ACADEMICIAN. I don't know how I could have been failed in French. After all, I covered three sheets. I developed the subject. I bore the historical context in mind, I gave a precise interpretation of the situation...at least, a plausible one. I didn't deserve a bad mark.

FRIEND. Do you remember the subject?

ACADEMICIAN. Er...er...

FRIEND. He can't even remember what he wrote on.

ACADEMICIAN. Why yes, I...er...er...

FRIEND. The subject to be treated was: 'The influence of the painters of the Renaissance on the French novelists of the Third Republic.' And I've a photocopy of your own script. This is what you wrote.

ACADEMICIAN. (taking the script and reading) 'The trials of Benjamin: After Benjamin was judged and acquitted, the assessors, not being in agreement with the President, revolted against him, assassinated him, and condemned Benjamin to the withdrawal of all his civil rights and to a heavy find of nine hundred francs...'

FRIEND. Hence nine hundred marks.

ACADEMICIAN. (still reading) '...Benjamin appealed, Benjamin appealed...' I can't understand the rest. I always had bad handwriting. I should have taken my typewriter.

WIFE. All that bad handwriting, those blots and crossings out hardly helped to put things right.

ACADEMICIAN. (still reading, after recovering the script from his wife who had snatched it from him) '...Benjamin appealed. Flanked by policemen uniformed like zouaves, like zouaves...' It's dark, I can't see the rest... I haven't got my spectacles.

WIFE. It has absolutely nothing to do with the subject.

ACADEMICIAN. But it has, indirectly.

FRIEND. Not even indirectly.

ACADEMICIAN. Perhaps I treated the second subject.

FRIEND. There was only one subject.

ACADEMICIAN. Even if there was only one subject, the one I did do was respectably treated. I followed it up and right through . I brought out each aspect, explained the psychology of the characters, threw light on their behaviour and demystified the significance of that behaviour. And the conclusion came at the end. I can't make out the rest. (To the FRIEND) Can you read it?

FRIEND. (inspecting the script) Illegible. I haven't got my spectacles either.

WIFE. (taking the script) Illegible. And my eyesight's good too! You pretended to write something. Just scribbled.

ACADEMICIAN. I did. I even included a conclusion. There it is, you see, in large letters: Conclusion or confirmation. They won't get away with this. I'll have the exam abolished.

WIFE. As you treated the wrong subject, and treated it badly, and put not much more than the headings, I'm afraid the mark was justified. You'd lose your case.

FRIEND. You would. Drop it and take a holiday.

ACADEMICIAN. According to you, I'm always in the wrong.

WIFE. They know what they're doing, those professors. They weren't made professors for nothing. They passed competitive examinations, they're properly trained and they know the rules for composition.

ACADEMICIAN. Who were the members of the Board?

FRIEND. For mathematics, Madame Binomial. For Greek, Monsieur Kakos. And for Latin, Signor Nero Junior, and others.

ACADEMICIAN. But they're no cleverer than I am, that lot! And for French?

FRIEND. A woman, secretary to the editor of the weekly review 'To-day, yesterday and the day before'.

ACADEMICIAN. Ah! Now I see! I know that wretched creature all right. She gave me that bad mark in revenge. I refused to join her political party. It was out of revenge. I have it in my power to abolish the exam. I'll ring the Head of State.

WIFE. Don't do that! You'll make yourself even more ridiculous. (To the FRIEND) Stop him! You have more control over him than I have. (The FRIEND shrugs his shoulders as a sign of powerlessness. To her husband, who has picked up the receiver:) Don't phone!

ACADEMICIAN. (to his WIFE) I know what I have to do!
  (On the phone:) Hello! The Presidency... Good morning,
  Miss. I want to speak to the President. In person. It's
  personal. Hello! Jules? It's me... What?... What's
  that?... But my dear chap, look here... But listen...
  Hello!...

WIFE. Is that him?

ACADEMICIAN. (to his WIFE) Be quiet! (On the phone:)
  My dear fellow, you're joking... You're not joking?...
  (He puts down the receiver)

FRIEND. What did he say?

ACADEMICIAN. He said...he said... 'I won't speak to you
  any more. My mummy's forbidden me to mix with the
  bottom of the class!' And he hung up!

WIFE. You should have expected that. All is lost. What
  have you done to me, what have you done?

ACADEMICIAN. When I think that I've given lectures at
  the Sorbonne, at Oxford and the American Universities.
  More than ten thousand theses have been written about
  my work, hundreds of scholars are pouring over my
  texts, I'm a Doctor Honoris Causa of the University of
  Amsterdam and the clandestine Faculties of the Duchy
  of Luxemburg! Three times I've won the Nobel Prize and
  the King of Sweden was astonished at my erudition.
  Doctor Honoris Causa... A Doctor Honoris Causa...
  and failed his bac!

WIFE. We'll be a laughing-stock!

  (The ACADEMICIAN breaks his academician's sword
  over his knee)

FRIEND. (bending to pick up the pieces) I shall treasure
  the pieces, in memory of our former glory.

  (The ACADEMICIAN tears off his decorations, hurls
  them to the ground and stamps on them)

WIFE. (trying to stop him and picking up what she can)
Don't do that! Don't do that! They're all we've got
left.

THE FOOT OF THE WALL

CHARACTERS

GENTLEMAN

LADY

1ST ENGLISH GIRL

2ND ENGLISH GIRL

YOUNG MAN

JEAN

RABBI SCHAEFFER

WOMAN

CONVICT

JUDGE

GUIDE

COOK

(Set: A high wall stretches right across the back of the
stage. On the far side, Audience Right, a very low door in
the wall. Pallid light. In front of the wall all the ground is
covered with withered weeds, almost dark brown in colour.
When the curtain rises the stage is empty for a few moments,
so that one can have a good look at the solitary wall, then
from the Left enter an elderly LADY and GENTLEMAN.
They are arm in arm and move towards the wall. Each is
carrying a black coat over the other arm and holding an
umbrella, also black. The LADY and GENTLEMAN stop in
the centre of the stage and contemplate the wall)

GENTLEMAN. It's an historical monument, 12th or 13th
    century. This world's full of historical monuments, 12th
    or 13th century.

LADY. I think it's Renaissance.

GENTLEMAN. I don't.

LADY. For seventy years you've been a member of the
    tourist industry...

GENTLEMAN. Not a founder member.

LADY. You've seen hundreds of monuments and you still
    don't know about them. Look at all those countless little
    holes in the wall. They were made by the bees so they
    could make their nests there, their bee-hives. That's
    typical of the Renaissance.

GENTLEMAN. They're holes without honey. In the time
    of the Renaissance the bees made honey there.

LADY. It's Renaissance, all the same. A dreary Renaissance, not so lively, a Renaissance in a twilight country. The Renaissance in Northern lands, or much further South, was far more gay.

GENTLEMAN. More like honey.

LADY. Brighter, sunnier. It always looks grey in the half-light countries, between the frontiers, in no-man's land.

GENTLEMAN. It's still beautiful.

LADY. You're wrong. It's not beautiful at all.

GENTLEMAN. I still find it beautiful. It's an historical monument.

LADY. I'd say it was a document in stone. A document's not always a monument. A monument's a more complex phenomenon than a document.

GENTLEMAN. It's still beautiful.

LADY. Our friend the Professor agrees with me. He knows better than you. He's a connoisseur. He knew this wall and he told us it was ugly, a monument that didn't come off. He knew before he visited it, he'd seen photographs in books. All those blocks of stone, just imagine, all so dark, where <u>did</u> they find them? This desolate square, all overgrown with weeds... All these withered plants growing from the hard ground, it's so neglected. Can you hear it cracking?

GENTLEMAN. Yes, it's caked mud, yes, it's the dry weeds. It all cracks underfoot.

(The GENTLEMAN bends down to pull up one of the plants)

LADY. (stopping him) Don't touch! Dried-up nettles bring you out in bumps.

GENTLEMAN. (turning to look at the monument again) The

monument's still beautiful.

(While the GENTLEMAN goes on looking at the wall, the LADY gazes round her. Then turning to the audience:)

LADY. The whole district's disappointing. What an idea to drop bombs on all the houses. Just gaping shells, blackened with smoke. Nothing but walls left standing, empty door frames, not a roof left, like huge teeth hollowed by decay.

GENTLEMAN. (turning round) That doesn't matter, no-one lives in those houses now. It was done for the tourist trade to give the streets a real period look.

LADY. And now it's raining. How damp the air gets all of a sudden.

GENTLEMAN. You know perfectly well the human body soaks up rain like a sponge. Put your raincoat on.

(They each put on a black gabardine raincoat)

LADY. Why are these gabardines so black? Once they were green, or yellow, I forget.

GENTLEMAN. I upset the inkpot over them. Even with pumice stone, I couldn't get the stains out. Then, so they wouldn't be noticed, I gave both the coats a complete soaking in ink. Perhaps it's because of these gabardines that everything looks to you so dark, so black.

(The LADY and the GENTLEMAN open their umbrellas, also black, they are both trotting along and sheltering from the rain)

LADY. How quickly the ground gets soaked! It was dry before, now look at it! And instead of being revived by the rain, the plants are sodden. The hard mud is getting soft again. I should have brought my skis. You're not making any progress. Come on!

GENTLEMAN. I still find that monument's beautiful, but I can't explain why.

LADY. Come along, dear. Don't get stuck in the mud.

(She takes him gently by the hand and seems to be pulling him along. They make for the wall at the rear of the stage, struggling through the slimy mud. When they get there, they stand with their backs to it, sheltering under their umbrellas)

Don't get stuck in the mud, come on, come on!

(She pulls him closer to her. From Audience Right two fair-haired GIRLS appear. They look alike)

GENTLEMAN. Look! Two young English girls!

LADY. Twin sisters.

(In spite of the rain, they are wearing flimsy white dresses, low-necked, with very short skirts and bare arms)

It's funny, they don't seem to be getting wet. (To the 1st ENGLISH GIRL:) Don't you need an umbrella?

1ST ENGLISH GIRL. No, Madame, we're natives of the country. The rain doesn't affect us. With you, it's different, you're foreigners.

(Goes on speaking. To the 2ND ENGLISH GIRL:) Just because you weren't allowed to become a dancer, that's no reason...

2ND ENGLISH GIRL. My one reason for living.

1ST ENGLISH GIRL. Still, he did give you lessons in gymnastics. That can take the place of dancing.

2ND ENGLISH GIRL. I'm not the one he's marrying, it's you!

1ST ENGLISH GIRL. Well, I can't see why that worries you, we're so alike.

LADY. (near the wall) The ground is dry here. (Almost

bumping into the two GIRLS) I'm sorry, Mademoiselle.
(To her husband) You've dirtied your shoes.

GENTLEMAN. Splashed with mud.

2ND ENGLISH GIRL. (to 1ST ENGLISH GIRL) That's no
reason, it doesn't stop me being someone else, not you.
I can't stand this position we're in.

LADY. (to the GENTLEMAN) She means their 'situation'.
She can't stand the situation. It's a more apt expression.

1ST ENGLISH GIRL. (to 2ND) You're not going to kill
yourself for that. What would I do without you? I'd only
be half myself. I'd only have one lung left and half a
heart.

2ND ENGLISH GIRL. You're getting married. Your husband
will lend you half his. I can disappear. I must disappear.

LADY. (to 1ST ENGLISH GIRL) Don't let her kill herself,
Mademoiselle.

GENTLEMAN. (to the LADY) Keep close to the wall. Look
straight in front of you, as though you can't see them.
Don't join in their conversation.

1ST ENGLISH GIRL. (to the 2ND) If you kill yourself, I
shall get cross.

LADY. (to the GENTLEMAN) Press your back against the
wall, you won't get so wet.

1ST ENGLISH GIRL. (to the 2ND) Yes, I shall be cross as
long as I live.

GENTLEMAN. The water's not coming down any more, it's
rising from the ground.

(The LADY and GENTLEMAN turn their umbrellas
upside down)

2ND ENGLISH GIRL. Here he comes, anyway. (The YOUNG

MAN appears from Audience Right) He loves you, all in all to one another. Where do I come in in this mix-up? You won't need me any more.

1ST ENGLISH GIRL. (to 2ND ENGLISH GIRL) Of course I will, don't forget we're twins.

2ND ENGLISH GIRL. That's what makes it worse.

LADY. (to the YOUNG MAN) Monsieur, your fiancee wants to commit suicide.

YOUNG MAN. It's not that one, it's the other one. You might think it's all the same, when they're twins, but I can see the difference.

GENTLEMAN. Marrying a beautiful young girl like that! Can it be true? Springtime, a miracle. The springtime of a miracle or the miracle of springtime.

1ST ENGLISH GIRL. (to the YOUNG MAN) Try and make her see reason, darling!

(The YOUNG MAN shrugs his shoulders. The 2ND ENGLISH GIRL runs off Audience left)

LADY. (to the YOUNG MAN) Stop her! (Crying after the 2ND ENGLISH GIRL, who has taken flight and vanished) Mademoiselle... Mademoiselle... Listen!

YOUNG MAN. She wouldn't want to hear a word, anyhow. And after all, I'm not responsible for all the suicides and murders in the Universe. (To the 1ST ENGLISH GIRL) Am I?

LADY. (to YOUNG MAN) You should have chased her on a bicycle.

GENTLEMAN. (to the LADY) Don't get involved in their affairs. Leave them alone - that's the custom in this country. One sister always dies for the other, or languishes away. It's a sacrifice that happens every day.

YOUNG MAN. (to the LADY) I don't have a bicycle. (He puts his arm round the waist of the 1ST ENGLISH GIRL) Do I?

1ST ENGLISH GIRL. She was exactly like me, darling. You could have kept your other arm for her. I'm just a little bit more plump.

LADY. (to the YOUNG MAN) You ought to save her, Monsieur. Not that I want to go against your traditions, but...

GENTLEMAN. (to the LADY) Leave them alone! You're being indiscreet. He's going to be rude to you.

YOUNG MAN. (to the LADY) Your taxi must be waiting. (To the 1ST ENGLISH GIRL) What would we do if I lost an arm? One has to keep one arm in reserve.

1ST ENGLISH GIRL. (to the YOUNG MAN) Up till now, you haven't. If the worst happened, then perhaps we could...

(JEAN enters from Audience left. He looks tired, but not so much as in the last episode)

JEAN. (seeing the wall) I knew it. Barring my way, making me waste time, when my hours, my seconds and my days are numbered. (He lays one hand on the wall as if testing whether he can move it or push it away)

1ST ENGLISH GIRL. (still with the YOUNG MAN's arm round her, to JEAN) Excuse me, I wonder if you've seen...

LADY. (to JEAN) Monsieur, I wonder if you've met someone on your way, someone who was running, I wonder if you noticed...

GENTLEMAN. (to the LADY) He couldn't. It was raining, sheets of rain.

YOUNG MAN. (to JEAN) No one can pass through that wall. It's a real one. At any rate, I couldn't. (He presses hard against the wall to demonstrate its solidity) It's not the only wall in the district, you know, but it's the biggest.

LADY. (to JEAN) Monsieur, please tell me. Didn't you meet a young lady running the opposite way, tearing through the sheets of rain, or come across her body on the road?

JEAN. (to the LADY) I did see a white cat rushing off...

YOUNG MAN. (to the ENGLISH GIRL he has put his arms round again) She's up to her tricks again - you see she's turned into a cat - the little rascal.

1ST ENGLISH GIRL. (to JEAN) Where was she going? Perhaps she climbed a tree and couldn't get down. Perhaps she went off and hid in a mouse-hole. (To the YOUNG MAN) At least, it's not as bad as if she'd killed herself. I feel easier about her.

LADY. (to the GENTLEMAN) You see, when you have a conscience... (To the ENGLISH GIRL) That's true, Mademoiselle. (To the YOUNG MAN) I'm sorry...

1ST ENGLISH GIRL. (to the YOUNG MAN) You have to understand her. I know her as well as my own reflection in a mirror which I used to confuse with hers. We must put ourselves in her place...

GENTLEMAN. (to the LADY) Well, if she's a cat, then... go on and find her for me quickly!

1ST ENGLISH GIRL. (to the YOUNG MAN) She was always sorry she'd stopped being a child.

GENTLEMAN. (to the LADY) Quick, go and find her for me.

1ST ENGLISH GIRL. Go and find her, Madame, perhaps she's having kittens. You can give me one and I'll keep it in memory of her.

YOUNG MAN. (to the ENGLISH GIRL) If you want to raise your sister's children, count me out! I don't see myself as their uncle.

GENTLEMAN. (to the LADY) Go and fetch her please, bring her to me quickly. A white cat is just like a bride. When I think of the time I've wanted one.

LADY. (moving towards the exit, Audience left) Yes, my dear, I'll do what I can. You know how much I want to make you happy. So long as she doesn't run too fast or I'll never be able to catch her up, with my legs.

GENTLEMAN. (to the LADY) Leave a message for her, anyway. Leave her a note under a big stone or in some ditch or other.

LADY. I'll do all I can for you...all I possibly can...

1ST ENGLISH GIRL. If she's turned into a cat, will she still be able to read, can she still recognize our symbols?

LADY. (leaving Left as fast as she can) Kitty-cat, Kitty... you'll get your white fur all filthy in the mud! The dogs will be after you! Come with me, come along and you'll be safe! (She disappears)

YOUNG MAN. (to the ENGLISH GIRL) When you stand there wringing your hands and take on that tortured look, it means you're only thinking of her. So go to her. She really was your better half, and you can never be mine. How can you expect me to live in a house where all your memories are hers?... You are not you, you're not a whole person, you live through her. Go to her!

ENGLISH GIRL. (to the YOUNG MAN, who is moving away) Stay with me, please! Don't you go away too! She left me because of you.

YOUNG MAN. I'm not taking the same road.

ENGLISH GIRL. Without you or her, that means no me, no us. I shall be nothing now, not even an apparition. (The YOUNG ENGLISH GIRL goes off on the Right) I have no strength left, I am without substance or support.

I shall go and lie down, alone, in blankets soaking wet, down in the lowest meadow, by the marshes, near the bowing reeds.

LADY. (coming on from the Left) My hands are all scratched.

GENTLEMAN. Was that the cat?

LADY. No. The wretched thing hid in a hedge. Through an opening in the thorns. It's the brambles that hurt. And scratched the cat too. There's red blood on her white coat. Come with me and we'll try and get her out, look after her and tend her wounds.

(The GENTLEMAN and the LADY go off Audience Left)

JEAN. (standing quite still near the wall, his back to the Audience) So I shall have to stop here. I can't stop. How can I get past, how can I climb over? I left the ladder at home, and even my pair of steps.

YOUNG MAN. (going up to JEAN) I could lend you my pocket-knife, Monsieur. That's all I can offer you. Just one blade. A bit uneven. But you can poke away with it if you have the patience. It takes quite a time, of course. That's why the blade's uneven. It's been used to try and get through other walls.

JEAN. With some success, I hope?

YOUNG MAN. Certainly not, Monsieur.

JEAN. Then how shall I manage?

YOUNG MAN. You are not required to manage. You just try, that's all. A try is a goal in itself. I myself have never tried to pierce this wall, or demolish it. I never even tried to climb it. I simply go round it, right round the building. I get where I want to go. I leave pockets of resistance behind me.

JEAN. This wall is the facade of a building. You have to know what's inside, whether there's someone inside or not.

YOUNG MAN. That doesn't interest me.

JEAN. I've got to know. That's the reason why people come from all the corners of the globe to visit historical monuments, to see them inside as well as out.

YOUNG MAN. You've got a mania for monuments, for museums and old churches. In fact, you never get inside them. You stand at the gates, or else at the foot of the walls. At least I don't create problems for myself. I've no intention of going inside. In our town the streets are fascinating. In the summer season there are tourists and other folk, lots and lots of them. We look at the tourists, who come to look at us. I don't look at them any more. One's enough as they're all alike except for a few differences such as colour and race, sex and size, age and status. I shall leave you, Monsieur, in front of your wall. It's late. I'm going to sleep. I put my bed up down there, under the apple-trees, at the water's edge, where the grass is fresh. Good-bye, Monsieur.

(He goes out on the Left. From the Left also enters a RABBI, quite young, with a black beard, a cassock, a round broad-brimmed hat and crimped hair. He is followed by little Jewish CHILDREN, very young, schoolchildren. There should be about twenty or thirty in a file if at all possible: two at any rate. Or else have puppets instead. They have black beards, round hats and cassocks. They march along in file, like schoolchildren)

RABBI. Eins, zwei, eins, zwei, links, rechts, eins, zwei.

(The CHILDREN march along singing very rhythmically, but the sounds they utter are not comprehensible.

The LADY and the GENTLEMAN enter from the Left, holding and supporting between them the 2ND ENGLISH GIRL, now a white cat, that is to say wearing a cat's mask and a white velvet dress, which covers her from neck to ankle. The white dress is stained with blood)

LADY. We are taking you home with us, Mademoiselle, we

are going to tend your wounds.

JEAN. (to the RABBI) Schaeffer. It's you all right, isn't it? Don't try and conceal it. I recognize you beneath your disguise.

SCHAEFFER. (to CHILDREN) Mark time! (The CHILDREN mark time. To JEAN:) It's not a disguise.

GENTLEMAN. (to the cat) We have an excellent Vet. He looks after the whole family. Looks after our doctor too. (All three move slowly to the Right)

RABBI. (to JEAN) From father to son, we have always been rabbi teachers.

LADY. (to the cat) You'll be nice and warm, and very well fed.

GENTLEMAN. (to the cat) And we'll make a great fuss of you. (They go out. The RABBI beckons and the SCHOOL-CHILDREN advance in their ranks, singing. The words all incomprehensible. They march right across the stage, perhaps marking time for a few moments, then resume their march and vanish into the wings on Audience Right)

JEAN. Aren't you afraid, with all those children of yours?... You might at least tell them not to sing so loud. Hymns and psalms are forbidden. You know where we are. You know here you are living in a country that is atheist, officially religion has been banned. Anyone practising a religion has his head cut off or gets sent to penal servitude.

SCHAEFFER. I know, I know.

JEAN. Their spies are everywhere. You're in danger. So, I suppose, am I, if I'm heard talking to you.

SCHAEFFER. Don't be afraid on my account, or on yours. I've pulled a few strings. I've fixed things with the powers-that-be. The police can't say a word. I'm not committing an offence. It's not psalms my children are

chanting, but passages I chose myself from the
Manifesto of the Communist Party.

JEAN. In that case, your offence is against your own
religion. You're fighting your own religion. You're in a
bad way, anyhow.

SCHAEFFER. I've foreseen every eventuality. There's no
risk where religion's concerned. I've had the passages
translated into Hebrew. My pupils are singing them in
Hebrew. That can't hurt their religion either, because
they don't know any Hebrew. You see? One can always
find a way.

(He disappears with the CHILDREN, still singing. JEAN
turns to face the wall again. He places his hands against
it and raises his head, but very calmly, without sign of
effort. The YOUNG MAN re-enters on a bicycle)

YOUNG MAN. I have come to keep you company, though we
have little in common. No serious subject of
conversation. The tourists have left. Schaeffer is already
far away with his children. They had to be hurled over
the precipice. Here we suspect people who play a treble
game. But Schaeffer will still get away with it, perhaps
with a broken leg. He's a man with lots of luck. Later
on he'll turn up again, in another country, as a ballet-
master, child-slayer, drunken husband, sentry or
gendarme. Or even, if things change - fortune's wheel is
always turning - he'll be managing director once more.
When he's not a tyrant on a big scale, when he's been
punished on account of his mistakes, his crimes, his faults
or the error of his ways, he finds some means of
becoming a little tyrant: schoolmaster, for example. By
hook or by crook he's just got to be bossing someone
about, persecuting someone, bullying or educating. If
he's just toppled over the brink, that means he's about to
change jobs. The precipice is our frontier. Beyond it is
another, more liberal country. Wouldn't you like to go
there? You should. You are a traveller. Wouldn't you like
to go down there? Though it seems that, after the
precipice, the ground rises again. You want to go over
the wall. Or better, knock it down. To know what lies on
the other side. A mania for knowing everything. There's

129

plenty behind that. Look at the people going by: there
aren't any just now, but there will be. You don't like
being in a field cut off by a wall? Walls are our
guarantees.

(JEAN still does not answer; he is still facing the wall.
He does not move. The YOUNG MAN speaks out loud,
but into space:)

It's risky, knocking the wall down. Anyway we'd have
to put up another one a bit further off. That would push
back our boundaries a fraction. The wall shelters us
from the Unknowable, from Chaos. Though only in a
manner of speaking. It's with us here, the Unknowable,
chaos. But it's a chaos we're familiar with, we've got
used to it. So I think I've tidied it up a bit, I think I
'know' it. And yet...who can stop the ground opening
under my feet? Who can promise me that the sky won't
collapse over my head? Think about it. If you can.
Meditate. I shall leave you to it.

(He goes out. JEAN still does not move. A WOMAN
comes in from Audience Right)

WOMAN. I had known him for centuries. He was tall. He
was strong. He protected me. Then he got thinner. Then
he lost his strength. Then he got smaller. Smaller
and smaller. Till he could no longer hold me in his arms.
It was I who held him, in my hand, in the hollow of my
hand. Then suddenly he vanished. (She opens and closes
her hand) I can't see him any more. Just imagine! You can
hardly believe it, such a fat man, so big and so handsome.

(While the WOMAN goes out, a JUDGE and a CONVICT
cross the stage)

CONVICT. But Sir, you are the presiding Judge. You've
sentenced me to hard labour, in perpetuity. That's too
much. It's out of all proportion. Besides, you will be
the loser. I shall never last out till the end of my
punishment. I'm sure to die first.

JUDGE. No, of course you won't! You'll see us all into our
graves.

CONVICT. If you let me out.

JUDGE. How could I know, at the trial, that you were my cousin? If you had said so straight away, the jury would surely have granted you extenuating circumstances. That's the done thing for families of diplomats, magistrates and typographers.

CONVICT. One can always come to terms with the Law.

JUDGE. That's what people say. It's not what they think. Look at it like this, when the Court comes to terms with the Law, there are special terms for special cases. First we choose four or five Laws at random, and then we select a few Special Terms. The same number of Terms as Laws. Then we put them all in the same shaker, and give it a good shake. Makes a funny sort of cocktail. It's never a success. Everything cancels out. No flavour of legality at all.

CONVICT. That's because you don't add enough salt.

JUDGE. What's salt for the defendant is not salt for the Bench.

CONVICT. What's salt for the goose isn't sauce for the gander.

(The JUDGE turns to JEAN)

JUDGE. That ought to make you laugh. You're very hard to please.

CONVICT. Let's get back to my case. What can you do for me? Are you going to let me rot away in prison?

JUDGE. You are in excellent health, I tell you. Are you in prison now? I see you're taking a walk in your uniform.

CONVICT. Only through an oversight.

JUDGE. You have very bad taste, cousin, to come worrying me like this. This is not one of my duty periods. Let me have a breather, can't you? Let me relax a bit. Let's talk of something else.

CONVICT. Very well. Do you like tennis? I prefer the circus.

JUDGE. I used to like the old-time circus. But lions and elephants are not the same any more. They're all donkeys now.

CONVICT. Neither are you or I.

(They go out. A MAN and a WOMAN cross the stage in the opposite direction)

MAN. We should have all the furniture cleaned in the flat. There's an armchair wants repairing.

WOMAN. It's all bound to get dusty after several years. However well you look after it, it's bound to get dirty.

MAN. At least we should have got something out of that furniture, shown it off to people, invited guests round.

(The MAN and the WOMAN turn towards JEAN)

You look as if you're taking a lot of trouble for nothing. You'll never be able to bash that wall in, or knock it down.

WOMAN. What good would it do, anyway?

(Confused sounds are heard: the rustling of trees, the cries of small animals, the twittering of birds, the burbling of a stream, and the noise of a motor vehicle stopping, to judge by the screeching of brakes. The coach stops. A GUIDE appears)

GUIDE. Ladies and Gentlemen of the Tour.

(The CHARACTERS conjured up by this image appear. JEAN sits down at the foot of the wall, looking apathetic, as though in a dream)

Ladies and Gentlemen of the Tour, we are going to halt

here for a moment. The next stop will be The Valley of Butterflies. In order to appreciate it better, we shall look down on it from the topmost peak. There, you see, if you follow my finger.

(All the SIGHT-SEERS gaze in the direction his finger is pointing)

In view of the length of the journey ahead of us, we laid on this brief halt for you here, to allow you a few moments in which to wash your hands in the stream burbling away so pleasantly at your feet. You have two minutes. Then, when I blow my whistle, you will start on the road to the summit. The coach will pick you up where the ascent begins.

(The TOURISTS all go off into the wings Audience Right. From the Left a tardy TOURIST appears, walking with the white stick of the blind. The GUIDE addresses JEAN)

Why are you staying here, sir? Don't you wish to follow the others?

JEAN. I'm not a professional tourist. I don't belong to the union. I'm a tourist in my own right. All on my own. At any rate, I'm not a member of your party. I'm not party to any party.

GUIDE. (to the MAN approaching) Come on, blind man, get a move on! Can't you see that the other tourists have gone on?

BLIND MAN. I can't see anyone.

GUIDE. (to the BLIND MAN) Hurry up! Go straight ahead and catch up your companions! (He turns to JEAN while the BLIND MAN makes for the exit. To JEAN:) One can't help wondering why some people travel. Do they ever know, themselves? Can't think what they can see in it.

JEAN. I know you, Mr. Guide, you are Schaeffer. You're back already.

GUIDE. (who should be played by the actor who took the part of the RABBI) What did you say?

JEAN. Schaeffer, you are Schaeffer.

GUIDE. I am not Schaeffer. You're mistaken.

JEAN. (quietly undoing the GUIDE's jacket and taking from the inside pocket a false beard) And this? You see, you can't deny it, you are Schaeffer.

GUIDE. (calmly, undisturbed) In actual fact, I am Schaeffer. Yes and no. I have been seen in so many countries and continents, looking so very different, in all sorts of disguises, that in the end people imagine that they can recognize me. Anyone who always looks exactly the same, gets lost in the anonymous crowd. His identity is ordinary, impersonal. It is my multiple identities, my vastly different disguises which show me up and give me away. That's because when you change, you attract attention. You break old habits and reflexes. Each time I break through into the norm, and as each time I am someone else, it goes without saying that I'm never entirely myself.

(JEAN, without speaking, points to the wall with his right hand)

SCHAEFFER. I know, you want to get through. I have seen you before and here's something you ought to know: when you saw me... God knows how long ago... going by with the children, I was on the bottom rung of the ladder. Now I'm on my way up. Soon I shall be a wolf or a lion again, but not too quickly. I don't want to fall, as my friend and I made the children fall.

JEAN. (absent-mindedly) What did you do to the children?

SCHAEFFER. We took off their little cassocks and their little round hats, we cut off their hair and shaved their beards, and then... and then we threw them over the precipice.

JEAN. Is that true?

SCHAEFFER. Oh yes... (Laughing) If you'd like to look
down there, down in the valley, there's quite a nasty
mess. I can see it doesn't interest you at all. Yes, I think
I have a few moments to help you to banish this wall.
It's not a good idea, but I suppose, well, as that's
what you want, I'll do it. I know that you know that I'm a
magician. Not the only one either. I warn you, you'll
have to go down and down, while as I told you, I'm going
up and up. (A brilliant light floods the stage) You see, it's
the sun. Austerlitz.

(Without any gesture from the GUIDE, the rear wall
vanishes. JEAN turns towards the back of the stage. He
advances towards the place where the wall has now
become a sort of dirty old kitchen, Audience Left, which
takes up not more than a third of the rear of the stage.
The walls are black with filthy dirty kitchen utensils
hanging on them and there is a dirty stove, black and
rusty. In the kitchen there is an OLD WOMAN with a
dark and dirty apron, a torn old black dress, holding a
blackened frying-pan which she is rubbing with an equally
black cloth. As the GUIDE goes off, Audience Right, he
takes a megaphone from his pocket and shouts through it
after the TOURISTS)

GUIDE. Gentlemen, friends, tourists and travellers, we
are off to the summit. (He blows through the megaphone
like a horn as he makes his final exit. The light follows
him out. When the GUIDE has disappeared, the last
section of the globe of the sun will have disappeared with
him. A greyish light spreads across the stage. JEAN is
left in the sort-of-kitchen with the OLD WOMAN)

COOK. That's your way, you'll get there, it won't take you
too long. You've more walking to do, still you're young,
you've a sound pair of legs. (She holds the cloth in one
hand and points with the other, using the frying-pan as a
pointer) That's the way, young man. Though you're not as
young a man now as all that. That's the way. (The rear
wall of the kitchen and the one on Audience Right open
to reveal two enormous gaping doorways. The kitchen
utensils, strung on cords, still hang across the openings)
Now you can resume your journey. We have removed
the barriers. But I warn you of the mud, the mud, the

damp earth that clings to the soles of your shoes...

(The remaining two-thirds of the rear of the stage reveals a very dark sky and a sloping ramp, which is of course hard to represent, as JEAN is at the top, about to go down the slope. It could be indicated by means of a few trees. The first one would be shown in its entirety, only the leaves of the second would be seen, and the third one would just reveal its highest branches and a few leaves beginning to fall, like the leaves on the other trees. Behind them an empty grey sky. Right at the back one distant peak, of which one sees nothing but the summit)

It's not nearly so tiring now, anyway, nothing like so tiring. No more uphill paths, no more mountains to climb, no more stairs to mount. You're back on the plain, my son, and then you go straight on, you can't go wrong... Off you go then, go on...

(JEAN is going out through one of the gaping walls, but turns round just before leaving)

JEAN. Your kitchen has no roof.

COOK. The clouds act as a roof. And the mist.

(JEAN goes)

JEAN. You never told me the way down was as hard as the way up.

COOK. No, I didn't. Maybe it is. It's a climb the wrong way up.

(You can see JEAN going, just the upper part of his body, then only his head. The COOK gets rid of her frying-pan and wipes her hands on her dirty cloth, which leaves black marks on her old arms and hands)

You can sing as you go. It makes it easier to walk. You have no heart for singing, you have lost your youth.

OTHER VOLUMES BY IONESCO

	Cloth	Paper
PLAYS VOLUME I (The Chairs, The Bald Prima Donna, The Lesson, Jacques)	£1.75	75p
PLAYS VOLUME II (Amedee, The New Tenant, Victims of Duty)	£1.75	75p
PLAYS VOLUME III (The Killer, Improvisation, Maid to Marry)	£1.75	75p
PLAYS VOLUME IV (Rhinoceros, The Leader, The Future is in Eggs)	£1.75	75p
PLAYS VOLUME V (Exit the King, The Motor Show, Foursome)	£1.75	75p
PLAYS VOLUME VI (A Stroll in the Air, Frenzy for Two)	£1.75	75p
PLAYS VOLUME VII (Hunger and Thirst, The Picture, Anger, Salutations)	£1.50	75p
THREE PLAYS		50p
THE BALD PRIMA DONNA (Typographic Edition)	£7.35	
PAST PRESENT: PRESENT PAST (Thoughts and Memories of Eugene Ionesco)	£2.50	

C AND B PLAYSCRIPTS

This attractive, but inexpensive series, is designed to present the work of both established and little-known play-wrights.

The current list includes:

			Cloth	Paper
*PS 1	TOM PAINE Paul Foster		£1.05	45p
*PS 2	BALLS and other plays (The Recluse, Hurrah for the Bridge, The Hessian Corporal) Paul Foster		£1.25	50p
PS 3	THREE PLAYS (Lunchtime Concert, The Inhabitants, Coda) Olwen Wymark		£1.05	35p
*PS 4	CLEARWAY Vivienne C. Welburn		£1.05	35p
*PS 5	JOHNNY SO LONG and THE DRAG Vivienne C. Welburn		£1.25	45p
*PS 6	SAINT HONEY Paul Ritchie		£1.25	55p
PS 7	WHY BOURNEMOUTH? and other plays (An Apple A Day, The Missing Link) John Antrobus		£1.25	50p
*PS 8	THE CARD INDEX and other plays (Gone Out, The Interrupted Act) Tadeusz Rozewicz tr. Adam Czerniawski		£1.25	55p
PS 9	US Peter Brook and others		£2.10	£1.25

		Cloth	Paper
*PS 10	SILENCE and THE LIE Nathalie Sarraute tr. Maria Jolas	£1.25	45p
*PS 11	THE WITNESSES and other plays (The Old Woman Broods, The Funny Old Man) Tadeusz Rozewicz tr. Adam Czerniawski	£1.50	60p
*PS 12	THE CENCI Antonin Artaud tr. Simon Watson Taylor	90p	40p
*PS 13	PRINCESS IVONA Witold Gombrowicz tr. Krystyna Griffith-Jones and Catherine Robins	£1.05	45p
*PS 14	WIND IN THE BRANCHES OF THE SASSAFRAS Rene de Obaldia tr. Joseph Foster	£1.25	45p
*PS 15	INSIDE OUT and other plays (Still Fires, Rolley's Grave) Jan Quackenbush	£1.05	45p
*PS 16	THE SWALLOWS Roland Dubillard tr. Barbar Wright	£1.25	55p
PS 17	THE DUST OF SUNS Raymond Roussel	£1.50	60p
PS 18	EARLY MORNING Edward Bond	£1.25	55p
PS 19	THE HYPOCRITE Robert McLellan	£1.25	50p

		Cloth	Paper
PS 20	THE BALACHITES and THE STRANGE CASE OF MARTIN RICHTER Stanley Eveling	£1.50	60p
PS 21	A SEASON IN THE CONGO Aime Cesaire tr. Ralph Manheim	£1.50	60p
PS 22	TRIXIE AND BABA John Antrobus	£1.05	40p
PS 23	SPRING AWAKENING Frank Wedekind tr. Tom Osborn	£1.25	45p
*PS 24	PRECIOUS MOMENTS FROM THE FAMILY ALBUM TO PROVIDE YOU WITH COMFORT IN THE LONG YEARS TO COME Naftali Yavin	£1.25	45p
*PS 25	DESIRE CAUGHT BY THE TAIL Pablo Picasso tr. Roland Penrose	90p	40p
PS 26	THE BREASTS OF TIRESIAS Guillaume Apollinaire	90p	40p
PS 27	ANNA LUSE and other plays (Jens, Purity) David Mowat	£1.50	75p
*PS 28	O and AN EMPTY ROOM Sandro Key-Aberg tr. Brian Rothwell and Ruth Link	£1.75	75p
*PS 29	WELCOME TO DALLAS, MR. KENNEDY Kaj Himmelstrup tr. Christine Hauch	£1.25	50p

		Cloth	Paper
PS 30	THE LUNATIC, THE SECRET SPORTSMAN AND THE WOMEN NEXT DOOR and VIBRATIONS Stanley Eveling	£1.50	60p
*PS 31	STRINDBERG Colin Wilson	£1.05	45p
*PS 32	THE FOUR LITTLE GIRLS Pablo Picasso tr. Roland Penrose	£1.25	50p
PS 33	MACRUNE'S GUEVARA John Spurling	£1.25	45p
*PS 34	THE MARRIAGE Witold Gombrowicz tr. Louis Iribarne	£1.75	75p
*PS 35	BLACK OPERA and THE GIRL WHO BARKS LIKE A DOG Gabriel Cousin tr. Irving F. Lycett	£1.50	75p
*PS 36	SAWNEY BEAN Robert Nye and Bill Watson	£1.25	50p
PS 37	COME AND BE KILLED and DEAR JANET ROSENBERG, DEAR MR. KOONING Stanley Eveling	£1.75	75p
PS 38	DISCOURSE ON VIETNAM Peter Weiss tr. Geoffrey Skelton	£1.90	90p
*PS 39	! HEIMSKRINGLA ! or THE STONED ANGELS Paul Foster	£1.50	60p

		Cloth	Paper
*PS 41	THE HOUSE OF BONES Roland Dubillard tr. Barbara Wright	£1.75	75p
*PS 42	THE TREADWHEEL and COIL WITHOUT DREAMS Vivienne C. Welburn	£1.75	75p
PS 43	THE NUNS Eduardo Manet tr. Robert Baldick	£1.25	50p
PS 44	THE SLEEPERS DEN and OVER GARDENS OUT Peter Gill	£1.25	50p
PS 45	A MACBETH Charles Marowitz	£1.50	75p
PS 46	SLEUTH Anthony Shaffer	£1.25	60p
PS 47	SAMSON and ALISON MARY FAGAN David Selbourne	£1.25	60p
*PS 48	OPERETTA Witold Gombrowicz tr. Louis Iribarne	£1.60	70p
*PS 49	THE NUTTERS and other plays (Social Service, A Cure for Souls) A.F. Cotterell	£1.65	75p
PS 50	THE GYMNASIUM and other plays (The Technicians, Stay Where You Are, Jack the Giant-Killer, Neither Here Nor There) Olwen Wymark	£1.60	75p

		Cloth	Paper
PS 51	THE MAN IN THE GREEN MUFFLER and other plays (In Transit, The Sword) Stewart Conn	£1.50	60p
*PS 52	CALCIUM and other plays (Coins, Broken, The Good Shine, Victims) Jan Quackenbush	£1.25	60p
*PS 53	FOUR BLACK REVOLUTIONARY PLAYS (Experimental Death Unit 1, A Black Mass, Great Goodness of Life, Madheart) Leroi Jones	£1.25	55p
PS 54	LONG VOYAGE OUT OF WAR Ian Curteis	£2.25	£1.05
PS 55	INUIT and THE OTHERS David Mowat	£1.50	60p
PS 57	CURTAINS Tom Mallin	£1.60	70p
PS 58	VAGINA REX AND THE GAS OVEN Jane Arden	£1.25	55p
*PS 59	SLAUGHTER NIGHT and other plays Roger Howard	£1.50	60p
PS 60	BLACK PIECES (Party, Indian, Dialogue, My Enemy) Mustapha Matura	£1.25	50p
PS 61	MISTER and OH STARLINGS Stanley Eveling	£1.75	75p

*All plays marked thus are represented for dramatic
presentation by:
C and B (Theatre) Ltd, 18 Brewer Street, London W1